300

D0898055

POWER TO PEOPLE

POWER
TO PEOPLE

The Inside Story of AES
and the Globalization
of Electricity

PETER GROSE

Island Press

Washington • Covelo • London

ISLAND PRESS is a trademark of the Center for Resource Economics.

Grose, Peter, 1934–
    Power to people : the inside story of AES and the globalization of electricity / Peter Grose
        p. cm.
    ISBN-13: 978-1-59726-172-2 (cloth : alk. paper)
    ISBN-10: 1-59726-172-6 (cloth : alk. paper)
    1. AES Corporation—History. 2. Electric utilities—United States. I. Sant, Roger W. II. Title.
    HD9685.U7A585 2007
    333.793'20973—dc22

Printed on recycled, acid-free paper

Manufactured in the United States of America
10 9 8 7 6 5 4 3 2 1

CONTENTS

INTRODUCTION

A "Green" in the World of Energy

By Roger Sant

The energy crisis of the 1970s stirred up waves of new thinking in American society and government. John Sawhill, dubbed the energy tsar of the period, called me to Washington not because of something particular that I had done but because of particular things I had *not* done. I had never worked in the oil, gas, or mining industries, had never set foot within the giant electric utilities. These sectors were the familiar sources of expertise, about the only places where anyone had given much thought to generating energy to power a growing society.

I was teaching finance at the Stanford Graduate School of Business, but I also worked as chief strategy officer of Saga Foods and had cofounded and served as chairman of a start-up high-technology venture in which I also had no special training or expertise. My primary credential was experience in financial management and, I like to believe, in thinking (as we later called it) outside the box.

But over those adventurous years, a different interest was pressing into the center of my daily life. The degradation of Earth's natural environment, from the stratosphere to Alaska's North Slope, had become a consuming concern for me. More troubling, as I looked around, was the fact that no one seemed to be doing anything creative or effective about it.

Washington, when I arrived in March 1974, was mired in the scandals of Watergate. One place where innovation seemed to be valued was the new Federal Energy Administration, which President Nixon had established and then left to its own devices as attention turned to his personal political destiny. Maybe here was a place where something useful could be done.

The team that I was asked to assemble worked to define policies to protect the environment and conserve energy, not to locate and consume ever more of it—just the pursuit that the old energy businesses scorned. This pursuit became my lifelong driving force.

I was naïve in the ways of Washington and politics. I started out by arguing moral and ethical imperatives. The futility of that hit me squarely early on, when I had to brief top members of the Republican administration about the plans we were evolving. After my (I thought) eloquent, professorial presentation, the ranking cabinet secretary responded with a one-word barnyard expletive. Thus ended the discussion.

Back to the drawing board. We worked up a different way of stating the argument. Conservation of energy didn't have to mean "doing without"; it meant simply using more efficiently what we already have. For all briefings to come, we translated the proposed investment to achieve energy savings into the cost per barrel of oil that we would no longer have to import from far-off and insecure sources. As long as using energy-saving measures cost less than producing an equivalent amount to consume, without sacrifice of prosperity and lifestyle, we thought we had a winning argument, touching the economic, political, and security interests of the people in power. Discussion resumed.

The concept of energy conservation has since become a mainstay in much of American society; back then, conventional experts considered it too radical for their comfort. Even now, three decades later, oil, gas, coal, and nuclear interests can summon powerful voices to declare the national energy policy as an effort to secure ever more sources of supply—instead of efficiencies, unsettling to all these interests, in the ways energy is produced and consumed.

After two provocative years in government, I was afraid I had done all I could. What I supposed I knew how to do, and wanted to do, was manage companies, the people and the finances that kept them going and growing. I believe that if government has a responsibility to protect our environment for future life on Earth, the task has to be shared with the private sector to be effective.

Not that work in the private sector is always gratifying. I knew from experience that companies can be as frustrating as government agencies for the people working there. I resigned from an executive post at one large company after just a year, discouraged because the man I reported to seemed to be the only one inspired by any thought of making the world better; all the others appeared more interested in their perks and status. Another company where I worked was almost destroyed by bickering among the founders. How rare it was to find corporate executives who just trusted people to do a good job.

Overall, I found that most people did not seem to enjoy their work and so did not give it their best. I was determined that it didn't have to be this way, and I had formed some ideas about what a good company should feel like: it should be a place where people *liked* to work, enjoyed the personal accountability placed upon them, where their daily effort would be appreciated, expanded, and built into a productive whole. This attitude seems self-evident now, but back then it was almost radical, unnerving in corporate boardrooms and chief executive offices.

In the late 1970s, some of the most promising energy policy reforms emerged in the industry of electricity—so long taken for granted, its workings so little understood. An obscure section of the Carter administration's policy became the opening to a momentous transformation, the restructuring of a closed industry that had gone largely unaddressed in federal policy making since the 1930s. And in the decade ahead, the forces of what would be called globalization revealed that the structural problems of providing safe and reliable electricity were not confined to the United States—they were fundamental around the world, particularly in poorer countries just embarking on their own economic development.

Needless to say, I did not anticipate all this when my family and I made the move from California, with its academia and start-up ventures, to Washington, DC, and the enterprise and politics of the Beltway. But the business corporation that came out of those naïve energy crisis years—we called it Applied Energy Services before shortening the name to AES—caught the wave.

Global electricity and AES remain works in progress, with spectacular ups and dismal downs. Projections are risky; the only constant is volatility. The undeniable fact at the opening of the twenty-first century is that people the world over need electricity and the services it provides. New generations everywhere are not prepared to do without those services for their daily well-being—and they shouldn't have to. The work of meeting that basic human need goes on.

POWER TO PEOPLE

ONE

Strategy of the Founders

The little venture that became known among giant energy conglomerates as the AES Corporation opened its doors for business the first day of October 1981, from rented rooms in the Rosslyn neighborhood of Arlington, Virginia, across the Francis Scott Key Bridge from Georgetown. Once a run-down community of pawnshops and used-car lots, Rosslyn was embarking upon gentrification, transforming itself into an office building complex inside the Beltway of Washington, DC.

At start-up, the company claimed no proprietary technology, no hard assets, no capital base. Its two founders, Roger Sant and Dennis Bakke, had no management record in heavy industry. They were not even clear at the outset about what their company's first "product" would be. All the young AES had going for it was a fortuitous opening to launch the free market in the old electricity industry, an entrenched monopoly ever since its creation nearly a hundred years before. The economic benefits of privatizing bloated regulated and state-owned industries were being argued around the world. Seizing upon a program of deregulation offered by Congress in 1978, the company's freethinking entrepreneurs set about to realize a vision of what private enter-prise is all about—or should be: to serve an important public need; to make a sustaining profit in doing so; to bring satisfaction to customers and employ-ees alike as they go about their daily lives.

Over the next two decades, their corporate experiment took a series of dramatic turns; it flourished in the stock market bubble, and it faltered, nearing the point of extinction, when the bubble collapsed. AES never sought the publicity of its competitor in the electricity business, Enron Corporation of Houston, nor did it suffer the subsequent fate and incur the odium that made the name "Enron" a symbol of corporate malfeasance and disgrace. The ambition that drove AES was, at base, the creation of a nurturing corporate culture that would allow all the people involved to do their best.

Sant and Bakke were Harvard Business School graduates from the far West seeking career fulfillment out East. Emerging from the federal bureaucracy during the so-called energy crisis of the 1970s, Sant had established the Energy Conservation Center (Bakke later came on board), sponsored by Carnegie Mellon University, to design an energy policy that could promote a growing national economy and, as well, enhance the lifestyles of generations to come. Excited by the possibilities they had discovered during their government and academic experience, they turned to the private business sector as the means to realize their vision of such a policy.

They incorporated their new enterprise under the name Applied Energy Services, Inc. (Eight years later, as they moved into the heavy industry of electricity generation, they shortened the corporate identity to AES—no superfluous and distracting periods.) Their purpose was modest, at least compared with what it later became: to offer their customers methods for using energy more efficiently.

"The typical energy consumer has neither the technological expertise nor the time or capital to concentrate upon energy efficiency, even when it recognizes the economic sense of doing so," they wrote in their first business plan. Instead of imposing on consumers "the burden of choosing between energy alternatives," they offered "a new approach which makes the provision of energy services the responsibility of a third-party specialist."

Choice of fuel—oil, gas, coal, or uranium; wind, wood, or the rays of the sun—was only one step, and not necessarily the most important. The equipment and management needed to convert raw energy into the many services consumers required were what mattered—starting with provision of the ducts, thermostats, and insulation and growing into the calculation of usage, the hours actually working versus downtime. "What is really important," they argued, "is putting together all the components in such a way as to minimize the total cost of delivering energy services." The third-party specialist, as they called it, was to be none other than the company Sant and Bakke presumed to establish.

Applied Energy Services, Inc., offered to identify, create, and market "innovative energy delivery systems that reduce the cost for energy services for major energy-using entities"—industrial firms and commercial buildings in particular, but even the giant utilities, which historically had not assigned a high priority to energy efficiency.

The important enterprise began, in short, as an attempt to elevate the idea of energy conservation into a profitable business—through efficiencies in the ways that energy was produced and then consumed. At start-up, Sant and Bakke presented themselves to corporate America as consultants in an untried endeavor. Sant called the concept behind it the "least-cost energy strategy."

It is difficult, nearly three decades later, to appreciate the novelty of this notion when it was first presented, so obvious and commonplace has become the practice of using energy efficiently.

Back then, "conserving energy" was branded a quixotic endeavor; it flew in the face of all the assumptions that energy industry economists had grafted onto the public and political awareness. To leaders of entrenched industries, the point of energy policy was—and for many still is—simply to secure access to more oil, gas, uranium, or whatever is required to shore up what they call the American way of life. Sant's argument to the contrary was that securing a reliable fuel supply was not the relevant or even the necessary goal of energy policy, neither for government nor for private enterprise. The more valid goal was to make better use of the energy already available.

The politics of the moment were not auspicious. The Republican administration of Ronald Reagan was coming into office, bringing the traditional assumptions of energy policy: the various industries are the experts, and their executives know more about energy than any professor. Sant's proposition risked oblivion. But the *New York Times* caught the drift. "Although the least-cost approach sounds simple," explained a business reporter in April 1981, "it represents a sharp departure from much energy analysis and the Reagan administration's overwhelming emphasis on fuel production. Under the Mellon approach, improvements in the efficiency of energy use are viewed in exactly the same light as increased production of oil."

The research team at Carnegie Mellon had generated data to demonstrate that, with improved energy productivity from the least-cost strategy, the United States could theoretically reduce its imports of foreign oil through the 1990s, as the *Times* reported, to none at all after 2000—without threatening economic growth or living standards. "While it's a physically feasible future," said a skeptical electricity industry analyst, "it's an unlikely future." He nonetheless conceded that the concept was "quite a good one." Other analysts were less charitable; one commented, "It's a lot easier to get off foreign oil in a think tank than it is in the real world."

Sant had published his first academic paper about the concept in 1979, after leaving government but well before finding the opportunity to translate his ideas into a business. During the energy crisis, he wrote, American consumers had responded nobly: "turned down thermostats, bought smaller and less comfortable cars, made fewer trips at slower speeds and joined car pools." But such sacrifices hardly went to the root of the problem, nor were they sustainable as a structural matter of energy policy.

"People simply want comfort in their homes at the least cost to them," Sant and Bakke would explain in briefings to prospective clients. "Similarly, industrial users need services like steam for chemical or refinery processes, or shaft power to run machines and equipment. They care little whether they use natural gas, oil, or coal, as long as they feel they are reliably obtaining the services they need at the lowest possible cost."

This change of focus to energy services rather than energy supplies allowed them to refute, one by one, assumptions that had been enshrined as established wisdom in the energy crisis of the 1970s and that, indeed, persist decades later.

Regularly heard, for instance, was—and is—the warning that the United States has become too dependent on imported oil, which is volatile in price and politically insecure in source. "Dependence on foreign oil is merely a symptom—a symptom of a much broader energy market imbalance," Sant and Bakke argued from their Carnegie Mellon post. "The belief that imports are the starting point from which all energy policy should flow is a myth, and perpetuating that myth will exacerbate the real problem rather than contributing to its resolution."

Oil may remain essential for transportation; ingenuity still falls short in devising practical and economical alternatives for gasoline or diesel fuels. "Yet, like the other energy myths, the focus on fuels results in misleading conclusions." For if oil and gas demand is reduced for other energy services, such as space heating and industrial processes, the aggregate volume and cost of the petroleum supplies still required for transportation services will naturally fall.

To the contention that energy is scarce, they retorted:

> While a scarcity of oil and gas is at the root of the present energy transition, there is no scarcity of ways to provide energy services. . . . Not only are substitutes for current energy sources technically available, many of them are less costly than oil, natural gas, and other fuels that have been considered essential and irreplaceable.
>
> While future economic growth will require growth in energy services, it does not follow that economic growth requires additional energy use. . . . The cost of saving energy through improving vehicle mileage and furnace and lighting efficiency is lower than the cost of most sources of energy supply. . . .
>
> Energy conservation and energy productivity mean the same thing.

Are higher prices for energy inevitable? So the experts warned the government and the public. Sant and his colleagues found, to the contrary, that competition among different systems directed to the end use of energy would actually reduce the cost of energy services to the users.

Business leaders and politicians comfortable with the arguments of the traditional energy industries complained that "environmentalists are causing the problem." But the Carnegie Mellon analytic models had factored in the costs of meeting environmental standards. In their briefings, Sant and Bakke declared flatly, "There is no basis to the argument that environmental standards must be weakened to meet national-security or economic-growth requirements." They proposed an alternative formula to measure the trade-off between environmental values and energy needs:

> Whether particular federal off-shore oil tracts or coal-mining lands are opened for exploration, for example, should depend on the perceived value of that land in its present state versus how much the exploration and resource extraction are likely to reduce the total cost of energy services.

Such was the flavor of the energy debate at the start of the Reagan administration as Sant and Bakke, both lifelong Republicans, sought to keep their contrary and unorthodox arguments alive. As it happened, support eventually came from across party lines.

The work of Sant's research team "is economic and factual—not a religion," said an energy policy maker from the retiring Carter administration, dousing the notion that energy conservation was something exotic. Then came a comment from David A. Stockman, nominated as Reagan's director of the Office of Management and Budget. Showing his familiarity with the academic literature and giving the concept bipartisan respectability, he stated during his congressional hearing that "we want to meet the energy needs of the country in a least-cost way." Within the decade, "least-cost energy" had become the common theme of state legislatures across the country.

Sant and Bakke continued exchanging ideas while completing the research project for Carnegie Mellon. In the practice of Washington networking, they kept up with like-minded people in and out of government—John C. Sawhill and Russell Train, on their way up to icon status in the environmental movement; Bill Hogan, later a professor heading the electricity policy institute at Harvard; and Dick Darman, who rose in the budget office of the George H. W. Bush administration and long afterward succeeded Sant as chairman of AES. From the earliest years, they knew, or knew of, one another and kept in touch. But for Sant and Bakke, in particular, there lingered the vision they devised after leaving the Washington bureaucracy: their own company, a place where they would *want* to work and where they could motivate people to do their best.

One early autumn day in 1980, Sant was driving Bakke back to town after one of those academic retreats where big ideas are considered and often forgotten. Under discussion had been a congressional initiative to reform the nation's electricity industry, and the established (and threatened) electric utilities were girding for a fight all the way to the Supreme Court. Cutting through the abstract discussion, Sant saw a practical opening. Turning to his colleague, he said, "This is our chance. Let's do it."

The partnership of Roger Sant and Dennis Bakke survived for two decades of AES, through triumphs and setbacks in the business of building a more energy-efficient electricity industry. In personalities they seemed an odd couple; their differing styles and priorities repeatedly caused tension within the company. Yet Sant could declare, "I don't believe a stronger partnership could ever have been created." The doors of their adjoining offices all those years were always left open.

Aged fifty, Roger Sant was courtly and soft-spoken. His kind manner (sometimes interrupted by flashes of irritation) inspired confidence even among those who could not quite fathom his abstract ideas about energy policy, much less grasp how radical they were. Dennis Bakke, his junior by fifteen years, a rugged blond of Norwegian descent, came on strong with the eloquence of an evangelical preacher in his zeal for doing God's will—not through charity alone but also through hard, competitive work.

Sant, an only child in a modest old Mormon family, was born in Los Angeles on May 24, 1931. His father had been accepted at the California Institute of Technology but had no money to attend; his mother attended the University of California, Los Angeles, for a year or so but had to drop out when the money ran out. Sant was a cheerful boy, without much sense of direction or intellectual stimulation, enjoying the usual newspaper routes and odd jobs for pocket money. He shrugged off his "average-mediocre" report cards in the public schools. Without much caring, he was admitted to Brigham Young University, where he supposed, still without much caring, that he might become something like a civil engineer.

Two years of missionary work was the defining rite of passage for a Mormon adolescent. After his freshman year at BYU, Sant was dispatched to an Oneida Indian reservation in Wisconsin, farther east than he had ever been before. His mission was to proselytize for the Mormon faith; a few months of that led him to think of a more down-to-earth undertaking.

Living with Oneida families who had broken away from their elders in upstate New York to make new lives, the sheltered young Sant concluded that what this lonely community really needed was not more numbers to add to their faithful. They needed a common home, a building to serve as a community center as well as a sanctuary for professing their new faith. With general approval from the church elders in Utah, Sant spent the next six months of his mission wielding hammer and saw to spur the Oneida flock into building their own little church.

In the years of his mission, he said, "I became an adult, more flexible, more tolerant, than from any dogma I had known as a child." Without ever openly rebelling against his Mormon heritage, Sant found his interest in the doctrines of organized religion dwindling. A changed young man when he returned to Brigham Young University in 1953, Sant found courses in economics and business and was academically stimulated for the first time in his life. He found excitement in dealing with real problems, case studies, the necessity of crafting specific responses to specific situations. He graduated from BYU in 1955.

On the recommendation of a supportive business professor, and to his own amazement, Sant was accepted into Harvard Business School. Enrollment was deferred for three years while he served in the navy as an intelligence officer on a carrier in the Pacific. When he finally arrived at that pinnacle of competition and prestige on the Charles River, a presiding academic dean issued him a stern warning: "Be ready for it: I don't think you're going to make it through here." As it turned out, Sant graduated in 1960 with distinction, in the top 10 percent of his class.

At Harvard, Sant found creativity in problem solving: problems have solutions, for those with the skills and energy—and the willingness—to look hard for them. Later, as financial officer for technology companies in California, he gained practical experience that he put to use in teaching at the Stanford Graduate School of Business from 1968 to 1974. He guided the basic business finance courses but stood back in fascination as his students launched into spontaneous discussions of the war in Vietnam, of the pros and cons of campus protests, of challenging authority: a new idea to a dutiful Mormon boy.

Sant and his family were nominally Republican, though he had never given much thought to politics in the abstract. This changed after 1968, thanks to his students and his new wife, Vicki Post. A Stanford graduate and a hotel executive, Vicki was passionate in her concern about burgeoning population growth and about environmental degradation in the North Slope region of Alaska. As he had in Oneida, Wisconsin, Sant began glimpsing a wider horizon.

The years of the Nixon presidency—a Californian in the White House!—lured more than a few westerners into going east; Roger and Vicki alike were attracted by the call of public service in Washington.

They arrived in early 1974, at the outset of the so-called energy crisis. Under pressure from the Organization of the Petroleum Exporting Countries (OPEC), the United States government was gearing up a new agency to coordinate policies relating to energy that had long been fragmented across government agencies. One of the pioneers of this reorganization, John Sawhill, a business economist, was deputy administrator of the Federal Energy Office. Sawhill quickly grew dissatisfied with the expertise pouring from the ranks of the oil and gas industries and the electric utilities, the only sectors that had previously given much attention to energy matters.

Sawhill was a shrewd manager, an outsider who could look at the field with fresh eyes—and he saw stark conflicts of interest. The makings of a national energy policy, in the outsiders' view, did not necessarily accord with the special interests of the energy industries and their suppliers. Sawhill set out to attract to the upper ranks of his new agency a cohort of smart business analysts, quick learners with no ties to the traditional energy industries.

Preparing a speaking trip out West, Sawhill asked his bright assistant, Dennis Bakke by name, to call one Professor Roger Sant at Stanford, about whom he had heard interesting reports. Bakke made the routine call and set up a lunch date for the three men in San Francisco. They had never met before. The upshot of that (in retrospect) epic luncheon was that on the day Sawhill was appointed administrator of the new Federal Energy Administration (successor to the Federal Energy Office) he offered Sant the post of assistant administrator. His charge was to analyze the possibilities for conserving energy and protecting the environment—exotic pursuits, at the time, in which complacent petroleum and utility experts had expressed no interest whatever.

As an apparent afterthought, Sawhill informed Sant that his deputy assistant administrator would be none other than Bakke. Arcane bureaucratic hierarchies were a distraction to almost anyone outside Washington, but even Sant was mildly taken aback when told who to hire as his deputy. He decided not to start off on the wrong foot by making an issue of it; Bakke was a pleasant enough fellow who seemed to know Washington—the ways of government, of dealing with Congress—far better than he did. "Thanks to Dennis," Sant said years later, "an awful lot of knives got me a lot less."

Dennis Bakke carried away no life-changing memory of that lunch in San Francisco with Roger Sant. If a newcomer to Washington would take him on as his deputy, that would be a big step up in the civil service.

Bakke was also a product of Harvard Business School, having attended a decade after Sant. His particular interest was in management theory and psychology, in making organizations work better. From his early years, he had been a zealot in motivating people to do their best. Whether it would be in government or in some company in the private sector, the implications of that zeal for his own life and career had not yet hit him. After all, he was but twenty-eight years old.

The middle son in a devout, close family of immigrant homesteaders in the American Northwest, Bakke was born on November 6, 1945, in the isolated Nooksack Valley, eighty-five miles north of Seattle. His father was a laborer, logger, trucker, and sheet metal worker; he remembers his mother as the more powerful of the two in intellect and devotion. Both sets of grandparents had come to America from Norway at the turn of the twentieth century. ("Bakke" rhymes with "hockey," the one sport that Dennis did not enjoy.)

Daily life meant work and prayer. The family's hand-to-mouth existence never kept them from welcoming foster children to their hearth. By the age of ten, Bakke tells, he had embraced his Christian faith as the driving force of his life.

But there was also the parallel value of work. It was one of the foster children who first drove that point home to him. Savoring a boyhood memory that he would often relate to adult friends, Bakke told of an after-dinner moment in the family kitchen. His mother organized the work of the household. The children scurried around clearing the counters, scrubbing the dishes, gathering up the trash, filling the wood box. A newly arrived orphan, three years old, sat in his high chair, absently playing with a matchbook car. Suddenly the foster child banged the tray with his little spoon and demanded, "I want jobs! I want jobs!" Bakke thus shared the origins of his conviction that meaningful work was the essence of self-identity.

Bakke earned top grades at Mount Baker High School, an hour's bus ride from home—though when he stayed late for sports, the bus dropped him off on the highway and he walked the last two and a half miles home. He was varsity quarterback, the basketball team's highest scorer, and prizewinner in the state public speaking competition, and he played first trombone in the marching band. Like most high school students, he dreaded the inevitable question "What do you want to be when you grow up?" It was Miss McGinnes, his math teacher, who put the question to him directly over a pick-up supper after football practice.

On the scale of career values for a Christian evangelical family, highest was always to be a foreign missionary, followed by a church pastor. Third was a service profession—social worker, nurse, teacher. Bakke allowed how he wasn't really sure, but maybe he should be a pastor or a teacher. Miss McGinnes shook her head. "No," she said, "your brothers are already committed to the ministry. Somebody will have to support them." The fourth level of career in this devout hierarchy was business, to make the money that would allow others full dedication to God's work. Bakke never looked back.

An athletic scholarship took him to the University of Puget Sound in Tacoma, 120 miles from home. He was the first in his family to go to college. After graduating in 1968, he applied to a list of business schools, ready to go wherever he could get a scholarship, a large scholarship. The best offer came from Harvard. When he reported this news to his father, the response was hesitant. "Where is this school?" the homesteading laborer asked. "What do you know about it?" After some moments of thought, he advised his son not to go. "It's too far away from home," he said, "and I've never heard of the school." Bakke graduated from Harvard Business School in 1970.

A student deferment shielded him from the military draft, but he sought a substitute tour of national service in the public sector—the federal government in Washington. Bakke was caught up in the enthusiasm and vitality of a younger generation dropped into the nation's capital. He found even the federal bureaucracy a challenging testing ground for inspiring motivation in a large organization. "Dennis was always high energy, never sat still, became really good at getting things done," recalled Bill Hogan of Harvard in an interview, one of the young crowd of those years.

Bakke's experience as Sant's deputy, and his growing expertise in unfamiliar energy matters, made a future in the private sector appealing. After all, Bakke's mission had been defined back in high school—to make enough money to support his brothers and sister. While driving through the hills of West Virginia one weekend in 1981, shortly after he and Sant had decided to found their own energy company, Bakke shared with his wife, Eileen, his expectation that they might soon join the ranks of the wealthy. He wondered whether they should establish a charitable foundation, to make certain that anything coming to them would be properly stewarded and shared. "But Dennis, you weren't even paid a salary last month," Eileen protested. Within the year, the Bakkes put together $12,000 for the first year of grants. A decade later, thanks to the business success of AES, the Bakkes' foundation was granting as much as $3 million in its best years, largely in small fellowships, to encourage faithful people in more than seventy countries to dedicate themselves to active ministry and Christian witness.

The Bakkes called their family charity the Mustard Seed Foundation. The image of the mustard seed came from the Sermon on the Mount: the smallest, most insignificant of all the seeds in the earth (Mark 4:30–32), "when it is sown, it groweth up, and becometh greater than all herbs, and shooteth out great branches," Jesus said. Then (Matthew 17:20), "Verily I say unto you, if ye have faith as a grain of mustard seed . . . nothing shall be impossible unto you."

During all their years together, Sant and Bakke never became close friends socially. They moved around Washington in different circles—Bakke found his after-hours enjoyment in his church, with its faithful congregation; Sant directed his social energies into environmental policy and advocacy groups. Asked often how they managed to work so well together, Sant would explain: "Not that we were two guys who saw the world in the same way. . . . It was almost because we saw it in different ways that we made such a strong partnership."

The story of AES, the company that grew from this remarkable partnership, is a story of the electricity industry undergoing a fundamental transformation in the last two decades of the twentieth century. It is a story of entrepreneurship seizing an opportunity in the fine print of complex deregulation legislation and springing into action. The wildcat venture moved in where the captains of industry, the rich and powerful old utilities, feared to tread.

The little company, plus half a dozen others following its lead, grew into a new global industrial sector. The economic strategy of privatization was catching on around the world. In country after country, the electricity industry ceased to be a protected monopoly, operating under government regulation and favor, and was thrown open to international competition among private enterprises. AES was nimble enough to adapt its business model to foreign societies, where, whatever the ideology or social structure, there was a growing demand for electricity, central to productive life and well-being.

But there is more to the AES story. What really drove the founders' partnership was a vision of good citizenship in the private sector. An elaborate system of corporate values took hold at AES; the tensions between these values and the pressures of managing a dynamic company in a competitive industry were an ever-present theme. AES was not a philanthropy; in the office, at least, Sant and Bakke were businessmen. Bakke used to say that profit is to business as breathing is to life; breathing is not the purpose of life, but should it ever stop, life would end.

AES was a profitable public corporation, doing well by doing good, as the sage Tom Lehrer put it. Anyone clever and confident enough to invest $10,000 when AES started would have been worth $58 million if lucky enough, eighteen or so years later, to sell out at the peak. As it is in the private sector, when the market bubble burst, those who were not so lucky lost much of the stake they had accumulated along the way.

When the founding partners finally went their separate ways, it was not because their aspirations and business model had failed. Rather, their company had enjoyed too much success, too fast. In the turnaround and recovery evidenced as AES approached its twenty-fifth anniversary, its story is a time line of growth, survival, and growth again.

TWO

The Power of Electricity

The phrase "energy policy" was being used in sound bites by the late 1970s, but it meant different things to different people. Was the primary goal of policy to develop ever more sources of fuel, as the energy industries argued? Or was it to encourage more efficient use of energy, as reformers worked to convince policy makers and the public?

Little appreciating all the elements contained within the sound bite, the Carter administration assigned "energy policy" top priority when it came into office in January 1977. By April, a package of complex policy initiatives was ready for submission to Congress, to face eighteen months of intense debate under pressures from special interests, from innovators and environmentalists to petroleum and utility lobbies—the latter, after all, with decades of experience behind them and billions in capital investment to protect.

Clarity of debate became elusive in the face of conflicting ideologies, competing visions springing from idealistic impulses versus habits and infrastructure. Should not, for example, government encourage renewable energy sources instead of environmentally destructive fossil fuels? Why not use wind power to turn the turbines of industry? Or capture the sun's heat in photovoltaic cells for space heating? Or develop fuel cells that could convert the virtually limitless supply of hydrogen in the atmosphere into consumable power? Energy professionals, comfortable in all they had built over the

decades, dismissed such alternatives, and they could readily cite early exper-
iments that had been disappointing on grounds of both reliability and cost.

The Organization of the Petroleum Exporting Countries' oil embargo of
1973–1974 had given daily-life substance to energy policy in the popular mind,
and that included top elected officials. But if dependence on foreign oil touched
all the political nerves, one of the most fundamental and enduring initiatives of
the Carter program turned out to be an obscure provision touching what seemed
to be only a subsector of the whole energy complex, the industry of electricity.
Scarcely understood and taken for granted by a consuming society, this industry was overwhelming in its infrastructure and committed capital.

Included in Carter's 233-page legislative package was a measure called
the Public Utility Regulatory Policies Act of 1978 (PURPA). The bulk of this
bill dealt with the kilowatt-hour rates that electric utilities could charge their
customers in a time of rising fuel costs. But buried within PURPA was the
inconspicuous Section 210, just three pages of opaque technical language.
Passing virtually unnoticed, this provision turned out to be the codification
of a reforming vision, a system for generating and supplying essential electricity at a lower cost to consumers and the environment alike.

Out of habit, perhaps, during the legislative debate the utility lobbies
directed their fire at the rate-setting sections of the bill, and by September a trade
journal, *Electrical Week*, was able to claim that their efforts had "scuttled or weakened . . . every substantive Carter rate-reform provision." Even a year later, in
November 1978, when PURPA became law, the utility interests had not picked
up on the point; the editor of *Electrical World*, another trade journal, assured electricity industry executives that PURPA "appears to contain no nasty surprises."

In their preoccupation with rates, complacent utility interests had not
looked deeply enough, for that modest Section 210 enshrined in law the
germ cell of a disruptive new business model for the generation of electricity. Roger Sant and Dennis Bakke were among the few to seize the chance.
PURPA opened the way to an overhaul of an energy industry that had grown
up in comfort from the first years of the twentieth century.

To Americans, thoughts of electricity commonly evoke the name of Thomas
Edison (if not Benjamin Franklin). Inventor of the incandescent lightbulb and

countless other devices to help people realize the promise of this strange new form of energy, Edison was an American icon.

Less remembered is the name of his junior partner and onetime private secretary, Samuel Insull, who never achieved Edison's mythic status. Yet it was Insull who devised the structure of an electricity industry that long outlived its creators. If Edison was never very good at business models, the diligent Insull summoned up the managerial and financial acumen that always eluded the inventor.

From the start, Insull embraced the concept of electricity as a "natural monopoly," an economic term of art defined at the dawn of the Industrial Revolution by the progressive British philosopher John Stuart Mill. No public benefit, Mill and his followers argued, would come from competition among suppliers of basic commodities such as water or heating fuel; each provider would have to operate wastefully, duplicating production and distribution facilities. Yet Insull was no robber baron monopolist; early on, he granted a role for government to oversee and regulate the business of supplying electricity. An epic deal was struck: in return for protection from wasteful competition, the electricity industry would be held to a high standard, a fundamental "obligation to serve" the public interest.

The pioneering partners differed in their business plans. Edison envisaged a system of small local power plants; he would point with pride to his pioneering Pearl Street Station in lower Manhattan, where, in 1882, 158 incandescent lightbulbs flashed on at the flip of a single switch! Maximum efficiency (and profits), he argued, would come from generating and distributing electricity to customers in the immediate neighborhood.

Insull had different ideas. He argued that large central power stations feeding current into long high-voltage transmission lines could supply electricity at lower cost than could local generating facilities. Economies of scale would better serve the public, Insull argued, and the more the demand for electricity, the cheaper would be its unit cost. This is the model that survived, and, given the technology of the times, the flaw in the plan went unnoticed.

Offering the electorate a New Deal in 1932, Franklin D. Roosevelt routinely invoked the name of Insull as a greedy monopolist. Yet once in the White House, Roosevelt championed the model of giant central power stations for bold New Deal initiatives such as the Tennessee Valley Authority and the Rural Electrification Administration. The electric utility industry complained that the entry of government upon its turf smacked of socialism, but Roosevelt's affirmation of mammoth central power stations offered legitimacy to their business model. In the post–World War II years of America's economic growth, the private utilities basked in power and prestige, deploying one of the most influential special interest lobbies in Washington and the statehouses. Growing consumption did indeed make electricity cheaper for all; economies of scale defined the electric power industry.

Not until the 1970s did Samuel Insull's business strategy show the first signs of crumbling. As the United States found itself increasingly dependent on foreign oil for its energy needs, including the generation of electricity, from this time on it would come only at vastly higher prices. Adding to the disruption was the new concern over environmental degradation, the damage to the atmosphere caused by huge power plants burning coal and other fossil fuels to generate electricity. Beleaguered managers of central power stations began turning to the alternative of "clean" nuclear power, which not only intensified the fears of environmentalists but also turned out to be not nearly as efficient or cost-effective as its promoters had promised.

Then appeared a sobering calculation from inside the utility industry itself: always before, economists could calculate that the more electricity was used, the cheaper would be its unit cost. That was the way it used to be.

Ever since Insull's days, prices for electricity had been determined by the kilowatt-hours delivered. The marginal cost, that is, the next-provided unit of electric current, was lower than the cost of all the kilowatt-hours that went before. The average cost of electricity, therefore, would fall. Hence came the economies of scale that supported the giant electricity monopoly. But confronted with higher oil prices, environmental cleanup, and cost overruns in constructing and operating nuclear power stations, additional kilowatt-hours delivered actually *increased* the average cost. The economies of scale had run out by the mid-1970s.

Atop this awkward economic reality came the long-unnoticed flaw in the "natural monopoly" theory for electric power. Edison, Insull, and those around them had assumed that the supply of electricity from generator to lightbulb was a seamless process, requiring a vertically integrated industry. The analytical scrutiny of the 1970s reached different conclusions: the provision of electricity was not seamless—it involved three distinct stages and three different businesses: the distribution of electricity to consumers; its transmission at high voltage, frequently over long distances; and its generation.

The stage closest to the consumer was called last-mile distribution: the poles along the roads and through the fields, and the low-voltage three-wire connections that hook into homes, factories, and offices. This stage might well be considered a natural monopoly; what sense would it make to have competing wires overhead and poles bumping up against one another? Feeding the poles and wires was the task of the middle stage, transmission of electric current over long distances from a power plant or substation. The business of transmission also might (or, it was argued, might not) turn out to be rightfully monopolistic.

It was the initial step, the actual generation of electricity, that demanded the bulk of the industry's committed capital and offered the greatest opportunities for reform. There no longer seemed to be a good reason why electricity had to be produced by a central power station. Maybe Edison's idea at Pearl Street was not so bad after all; a small nearby generating plant might do the job just as cheaply and with less environmental damage. It might even use those "exotic" alternative fuels—solar, wind, wood, biomass in general—that the giant utility managers dismissed as too small and troublesome even to consider.

The 1970s also brought forth the general business concept of "disruptive technology." This meant devices and processes that were underestimated at first but gained acceptance and took industry strategists by surprise; companies unwitting or unprepared would be unsettled, even destroyed. (Home copiers and personal computers remain prime examples of disruptive technologies.) "Initially neglected by the companies that dominate a given market, and that are heavily invested in the existing infrastructure," as one analysis summed up the concept, "the invading technologies are often spearheaded by hungry newcomers who gain early footholds and grow at steep trajectories, eventually pushing aside the market leaders."

In 1980, Sant and Bakke were hungry newcomers. Only gradually, as the "disruptive" provisions hidden within PURPA survived court challenges by the utility industry, did the openings become real.

For all its opaque formulation, Section 210 encouraged a new industry sector of independent power-generating companies to supplement, if not yet replace, the utilities' central power stations. At first, the entrepreneurial power generators could sell their output only to the regulated utilities, but at an attractive price called the "avoided cost"—the cost the utilities avoided by not building and operating new power plants themselves. This business soon evolved into a competitive free-market environment, with the independent unregulated producers offering their output to any buyer, in contractual long-term or spot transactions.

It was the avoided cost, a principle mandated in statute, that gave AES and the other independent producers their opening onto a spectacular growth curve. These upstart companies could be more flexible than the large utilities in siting and modular construction, over shorter lead times and with smaller capital requirements, yet would have greater incentives for operating efficiently. They estimated undercutting by as much as 15 percent the cost of electricity produced by the cumbersome central power stations. Independent power producers could reap returns, for instance, from mass production of generating equipment. Instead of requiring massive custom-built machinery, smaller plants would operate with standardized turbines and related devices produced on assembly lines. Jet engines designed for fleets of aircraft could be readily adapted to drive the turbines of small power producers. The revenues made possible by the avoided costs led to extraordinarily, indeed embarrassingly, high profits, which provoked years of tedious litigation.

Section 210 went even further to encourage the restructuring. The statute recognized that, to be meaningful, new independent generators must have entry access to the regional transmission lines, the middle stage in the supply of electricity. They must be able to insert their output, in quantities large or small, into the grid. Grid engineers, controlled by the giant utilities, spurned contributions from small independent generators, arguing that their output was too insignificant to matter and that the quality control necessary for the grid's reliability would be compromised.

Both reservations grew specious during the 1970s. If the output of any one or two of Edison's Pearl Street power stations would indeed be trivial to the vast grid (158 lightbulbs within a nationwide network?), hundreds or thousands of such independent generators would reach significant volume. Quality control issues were readily solved once the self-protective utilities managing the grid were forced to devise secure and efficient means of access.

On the point of grid access, the terms of PURPA were both specific and mandatory: to meet fluctuating demand, utilities were *required* to buy any electric power proffered to the regional transmission lines, and at a unit price equivalent to what it would have cost them to increase their own generating power.

Finally, hidden within PURPA was yet another "nasty surprise": to ensure that entrenched utilities did not move to preempt the new hypothetical and unregulated industry sector, the statute ordered that no regulated utility could own a controlling interest in an independent power-producing company.

Utility interests took to the courts to block the PURPA provisions they had overlooked while flexing their muscle in Congress. They filed two legal challenges, one to the strategy of deregulation, the other to the avoided costs that utilities would have to pay the rude upstarts, the independent power producers. In both cases, lower courts sided with the utilities.

In both cases, the United States Supreme Court reversed the lower courts' decisions, in June 1982 and May 1983. The mandated price would not necessarily lead to cheaper electricity for consumers, the high court conceded, but it would further the intent of Congress to encourage alternative energy technologies and efficiency, reducing dependence on fossil fuels.

The radical provision of PURPA's Section 210 became the law of the land. Vertically integrated utilities could no longer exclude independent power producers, competitive and unregulated, from their protected closed systems. Insull's natural monopoly was broken wide open.

"It was like the birth of a new galaxy!" declared John McArthur, dean of Harvard Business School and longtime director of AES in an interview looking back upon two decades of the independent power industry. The rhetoric soared to the cosmos: stellar systems, a fusion of forces, intragalactic behavior, all took form; it was a moment to journey into the inchoate, a time for a new creation!

Back down on Earth were the old fundamentals. Plodding electric utilities saw their light dimmed by the meteoric attack of the 1990s investment boom, just as the unregulated sector was forming into a star. New companies generating and trading electricity emerged as popular growth stocks. AES, Enron, and the others became darlings of investment fund managers and shareholders seeking spectacular capital gains. Dramatic growth in earnings, which Sant and Bakke confidently projected, seemed destiny for years into the future. Even the traditional utilities started making peace with the disruptive new sector as they saw the benefits of new liquidity in the electricity marketplace.

Cosmologists say that the fundamental features of a universe are determined in the first seconds of creation. Any company created by Sant and Bakke, accordingly, would be a friendly place to work; from the start AES had some of the character of a family business.

Bakke interviewed an applicant, Leith Mann, for a job as his secretary. On first meeting, their introductory smiles suddenly turned into laughter: both of them, aged thirtyish, had shiny braces on their teeth. Bakke hired Mann on the spot; she rose in AES to become an officer of the company. Sant tried to sign up all the principals of the Carnegie Mellon Research Institute for his new company, but given the slow pace of raising capital, some of the key people, including the developer of the first databases, backed away.

Employee number five, according to her AES ID card, was a young Wesleyan University graduate (class of '79) named Sheryl Sturges who had designed an all-solar house as an undergraduate project and then had earned an MBA from George Washington University in management of science, technology, and innovation. Sturges was the daughter of an ecologist, and her husband was an activist in the cause of addressing world hunger who, as such, had become acquainted with an eclectic business executive turned energy analyst named Roger Sant. She was hired to help adapt the data of the least-cost energy strategy for individual clients and subscribers, and she went on to design some of the company's most innovative environmental endeavors.

At a Washington Halloween party in 1981, Sant had bumped into Ken Woodcock, one of his former deputies in the Federal Energy Administration, a mechanical engineer with a business school degree. During a tour of duty with the U.S. Public Health Service, Woodcock had learned about air pollution and related issues that in those years few others understood. He was about to leave government for the private sector and casually inquired whether there might be a place for him in Sant's start-up energy company. Sant did not want to make a definite offer without the concurrence of his cofounder, but Bakke was not at the party and could not be reached; he was running the next day in a Washington marathon. Early the next morning, Sant pulled on his tennis shorts, hoping they could pass muster in running a marathon, and contrived to join the race unofficially just as Bakke was going by. For a mile or so they ran together as Sant explained how Woodcock might fit in. Bakke, conserving his breath for the task in play, said, "Sure."

"I sat in the hallway and ran the computer," Woodcock recalled. "There were no job areas and no job descriptions." And, as Sant had warned him from the start, there was no money for a payroll; Woodcock began his career at AES as a volunteer. He quickly took charge of exploring business opportunities as the start-up gained momentum, and he served as a top executive for more than twenty years.

Another early recruit was Roger Naill who had earned his PhD with a dissertation about the art of energy forecasting; so shrewdly did he dissect the Carter administration's energy policy that he was promptly offered a job with the U.S. Department of Energy, cabinet-rank successor to John Sawhill's fledgling agency. Naill and Sant met from time to time at policy conferences. Sant saw in him the expert who could meet the analytical and conceptual demands of clients requiring custom-tailored energy services. "I accepted the job on blind faith," Naill conceded. He and Sturges managed the consulting business of Applied Energy Services, providing revenues and cash flow for the start-up company's first five years as it defined a grander operating role for itself in the new era of independent power producers.

This was the core team present at the creation of AES. From the start, Sant and Bakke fell into naturally complementary roles in the Arlington office. "Roger is a visionary," remembered Leith Mann. "He can make anyone feel at ease; people are his forte. Dennis recognizes the essence of complicated things and makes them understandable." Bakke concentrated on managing the company; he called himself the inside man. Sant was the out-side man, lunching with corporate executives and government officials, turn-ing on his persuasive manner to ferret out creative business opportunities that might improve people's lives and turn profits at the same time. Sant's nim-ble mind substituted for a glaring lack of expertise in engineering matters: for all his insights into energy policy, he knew next to nothing about how electricity actually came about.

In fact, absence of expertise was not all that extraordinary in the practi-cal business of electricity. Edison himself once confessed, "At the time I exper-imented on the incandescent lamp I did not understand Ohm's Law." Slyly disingenuous from his later loft of eminence, he added: "I do not *want* to understand Ohm's Law—it would prevent me from experimenting."

After three months of consulting, with just one paying client under contract, Applied Energy Services reported year-end revenues for 1981 of $125,000 and outstanding debt of $115,000. Net worth for the company adjusted out at $7,000 in a bank account. Sant and Bakke took out personal loans to cover immediate overhead.

They sought serious start-up capital in a private equity offering managed by the investment banking partnership of L.F. Rothschild, Unterberg, Towbin (Tom Unterberg joined Sant on the little company's board as the first outside director and served for two decades). The offering went to a small number of financial institutions and sophisticated investors, who had to certify their capacity to absorb a total loss; as with most ventures of the period, no one with less than $1 million in net worth need apply.

To this select group, Applied Energy Services described an audacious business plan to seize upon the opportunities opened by PURPA, still pend-ing before the Supreme Court, to design, build, and operate electric power plants more efficient, economical, and environmentally sound than any known before. They proposed to "structure and participate in joint ventures, limited partnerships and similar vehicles" to bring into operation self-sustain-ing companies to generate electricity independently of the regulated utilities, competing in an unregulated free-market environment.

Potential investors were left in no doubt about the speculative nature of the venture. Among pages of "risk factors" in the offering statement was an ominous warning: "None of the management group has been involved in business in the company's proposed operations area. Also, other than Mr. Sant, none of the management group has significant experience in starting up or managing an enterprise similar to the company."

The offering raised $1.2 million in start-up capital early in 1982, largely from the underwriting partners, Sant himself, and Sant's father and uncle. This fell short of the $3 million they had hoped to raise, but it was better than personal loans to launch a growth trajectory.

The pioneering investors were on notice to expect a $600,000 operating loss in 1982, the company's first full year in business; when the returns came in, the actual loss was just $355,000, on total revenues of $1.13 million. Sant and Bakke expressed confidence that Applied Energy Services would break even and achieve profitability by the second quarter of 1983— not bad for a speculative start-up.

On the horizon as it expanded, their company's real prospect was taking shape.

THREE

Into Deep Water

In granting statutory authority for new independent power-generating companies, Congress took the unusual step of writing into the legislation generous provisions regarding one innovative technological process, enthusiastically promoted in President Carter's national energy policy. It was called cogeneration.

The theory was simple and beguiling. Electricity is generated from a rotating turbine, generally driven by the pressure of steam produced from water heated to the boiling point. That is what happens inside a power plant. To energy policy reformers seeking greater efficiency in production and use, it seemed an obvious waste to release the driving steam into the air after it had finished its "day job" pressing against the blades of the turbine. Why not capture the "waste product" and deliver it to a nearby factory or office building, which could use the steam for space heating, refrigeration, or its own industrial processes—in effect drawing double duty from the same consumption of primary fuel?

"Industrial firms that consume substantial amounts of electricity and also require steam in their operations typically purchase electricity from an electric utility and independently generate their own steam using on-site boilers," Roger Sant and Dennis Bakke explained in their first prospectus. Instead, they proposed, "many industrial plants could satisfy their electricity and steam needs at less cost through an on-site cogeneration system which, for example, produced both electricity and steam (or hot water) by using the heat from the waste exhaust in the electricity generation process to make the steam (or hot water)."

Engineers of cogeneration argued that a streamlined design, even burning fossil fuels under tight environmental safeguards until alternative, renewable fuels became practical, could be cost-effective. If a traditional power plant achieved only 30–35 percent efficiency (the electricity produced against the energy first consumed), a typical cogeneration plant showed promise of achieving twice that efficiency.

Applied Energy Services, Inc., started as a consulting business, providing energy-efficient solutions for commercial and industrial consumers. But the founders' goal stretched far beyond consulting. They sought to make the visionary technology of cogeneration into the operational reality of a competitive, profitable business.

Sant's job in the opening months was to visit corporate boardrooms and industrial installations around the country to stir up interest in his company, clients for his least-cost energy strategy, and, more eagerly, customers and settings for new state-of-the-art cogeneration plants.

A natural early contact was the giant oil company ARCO (formerly the Atlantic Richfield Company, later BP). From its president, William F. Kieschnick, who had chaired Sant's advisory board at Carnegie Mellon's Energy Conservation Center, Sant learned of a troublesome oil refinery that ARCO operated along the Houston Ship Channel, one of the world's largest industrial complexes. Its salient feature was an ungainly pile of petroleum coke laced with sulfur, a polluting waste product of the oil-refining process that ARCO was trying to sell off for a fraction of its potential energy value. For anyone interested in energy efficiency and technological fixes for pollution, here was a challenge.

Sant's penchant for experimental thought went to work. As he later admitted, he had not the slightest idea what petroleum coke was, but he had heard of it when he served as a board member of the dynamic Thermo Electron Corporation under his friend and mentor in technology innovation George

Hatsopoulos. (At one point, Sant had offered AES as a potential Thermo Electron subsidiary, but Hatsopoulos instead chose to make a minority investment in Sant's company.) Waxing eloquent to ARCO executives, Sant proposed the notion of pulverizing the troublesome stuff to fuel a mighty slow-speed diesel engine (the kind used on large ships), which would in turn drive the turbines of a new power plant. Waste coke thus would produce useful electricity. Diesels were high in energy efficiency, but when burning a dirty fuel such as petroleum coke they also produced noxious emissions, and the cleanup cost threatened to negate the savings from diesel technology. Nonetheless, ARCO's creative head of research, Armin Baertschi, had faith in Sant and put up $25,000 to start the project. Sant and Bakke brought in Robert F. Hemphill Jr., another former deputy in the federal energy bureaucracy, to manage planning of the pioneering venture, which they named AES Deepwater.

Years later, Hemphill told Robert H. Waterman Jr. of McKinsey & Company, an early AES advisor, "It was the screwiest idea the world had ever heard. We were going to try to grind petroleum coke, mix it with water, inject it into diesels, and then try to clean up the exhaust. How we ever got ARCO to suspend disbelief is to Roger's credit. Even in Waring blenders, we couldn't have mixed that fuel."

Pulverized coke could theoretically fuel slow-speed diesel engines, feasibility studies showed, but if a boiler had to be added to clean up the diesel exhaust, why not skip the diesel stage and just burn the petroleum coke in the boiler directly? The resulting steam would turn the turbines to generate the electricity and could then be captured as exhaust for a second industrial use: cogeneration—just what the PURPA statute and the independent power-generating companies envisaged.

More environmental consequences intruded: coke, as Sant finally learned, contained almost 8 percent sulfur; the dirtiest coal registered a sulfur content of only 0.5–3 percent. Sulfur dioxide caused acid rain. A technological fix using "scrubbers" could be used, wherein the sulfurous emissions would be mixed with limestone to eliminate sulfur dioxide—except that the scrubbing process itself produced a stream of wet and dirty calcium sulfate, not a hazardous substance but a problem for solid waste disposal.

Sant learned of a process to convert calcium sulfate into pure gypsum, a commodity of value. And—the entrepreneurial imagination soared—near the proposed Deepwater power plant was a wallboard factory that could well use a convenient source of the raw material. Disillusionment followed, however, in the kind of problem that plagued so much energy innovation in these early years: conversion would cost more than the gypsum at market price. If Sant and Bakke were to honor their professed dedication to sound environmental practices, there was no choice but to go ahead with the scrubbing and conversion process. (As it turned out, the gypsum part of the system did not drain cash-flow resources as feared.)

All through 1983, Sant, Bakke, and Hemphill worked with the Bechtel Corporation on plans for a showpiece facility to extract energy from a huge, ugly pile of petroleum waste coke. The local utility, the Houston Lighting & Power Company, was ready to contract for the electricity. ARCO's oil refinery not only would supply the fuel but also could use the steam. Deepwater would become a 140-megawatt power plant, generating enough electricity to serve 140,000 people and producing 30,000–600,000 pounds of steam per hour for the refinery. It would cost $275–$280 million to build, a modest cost compared with that of the usual central power station but daunting to a company that two years before had just $7,000 in its checking account.

With their analytic expertise and infectious enthusiasm, Sant and Bakke managed to attract the attention of business giants: ARCO was an obvious, if wary, partner; so was Bechtel, which would win the contract to build the plant. Nine large creditors, led by J. P. Morgan and the General Electric Credit Corporation, provided lease financing.

A legal deadline loomed before the enterprise: December 31, 1983, expiration date of antipollution tax credits for new industries in Texas. During three months of virtually marathon negotiations among thirteen diverse partners, each pursued its own agenda and harbored its own doubts. Last-hour problems were resolved in around-the-clock negotiations, and Sant, Bakke, and Hemphill secured the final signatures at 4:31 p.m. on December 30, just in time for the funds to be transferred in advance of the deadline.

"Suddenly, we were real," declared an awestruck Sant, "a real business." For the rest of his decades as head of AES, he would express gratitude to that handful of bankers, lawyers, and engineers, "individuals willing to take a stand, . . . who took a great personal risk" to get the project under way. Bakke said of Deepwater, "We did something that had never been done before, in a way that had never been done."

Fees from least-cost energy consulting and the designing of Deepwater mounted. Applied Energy Services reported a consolidated net income of $919,000 for 1983, compared with a loss of $355,000 the year before.

Construction of the Deepwater cogeneration plant began in February 1984; a mere eighteen months later, the plant was ready to begin start-up tuning. The first fire was set in the boiler in December, and the turbine started to turn in February 1986, reaching full load by May. Commercial operation began on June 27, 1986. At full speed over years to come, AES Deepwater achieved a remarkable record of operational safety and efficiency, recording emissions of sulfur dioxide and nitrous oxide more than 50 percent *below* established environmental standards.

That was the good part. Troubles came from the financing package that had been so boldly cobbled together. As industry and consumers have learned with pain, the price of energy is subject to alarming and sudden volatility. A decade later, Hemphill himself told a scary story at an orientation meeting for new AES employees: "Some idiot signed a power contract that tied the price of electricity directly to the price of natural gas." By then, the spirit of a good-natured family company had come to define the AES culture. Savoring a dramatic pause in his presentation, the founding project director went on, "That meathead is sitting right here talking to you."

As it happened, contrary to projections, the price of natural gas tumbled in the late 1980s, and Deepwater had to sell its electricity at a rate much lower than expected. Revenues in the early 1990s amounted to $20 million, enough to operate the plant efficiently and safely but not to cover the mounting debt service. After four years of successful operation, Deepwater was, as a practical matter, bankrupt. Not until January 1995, after sometimes acrimonious negotiations to restructure the original debt, did AES manage to buy out the initial creditors (at a large discount) and secure sound financial footing.

Electric power plants are an ever-present and unappreciated fixture on the landscape of industrial society. AES, along with the other independent power producers, even if granted the best of intentions, finds it almost as hard as the old utilities to make its power plants things of beauty in the community.

Dominating the scene are towering smokestacks, designed to dispel exhaust gases high enough to protect the air quality of nearby neighborhoods. Rattling conveyor belts rise at awkward angles from ugly piles of coal and limestone. Ungainly ducts direct steam from building to building. Webs of wires and insulators connect to underground cables to deliver electric current to the grid substation. Despite all attempts at beautification, including imaginative landscaping and soothing pastel paint, power plants seem to end up looking like some precocious child's Erector set.

Neighbors may raise the battle cry "Not in my backyard!" even as they insist on the services, plentiful and reliable, that the plant is built to provide. Few have any understanding of, or even curiosity about, what goes on inside the plant or why it had to be placed within view.

Sant made some headway toward analytic clarity when, in his first academic writings, he argued the now evident point that electricity is just another commodity, "similar to, for example, primary foodstuffs, metals or forest products that are also incorporated into finished goods and used by consumers."

But the commodity concept brought up two complications, given that electricity differs from other commodities. First, in contrast to the familiar agricultural products that have served human societies from the beginning, electricity seems to offer no benefit in its own right. Its raw, natural form—we see it as lightning—is frightening and often destructive. Benjamin Franklin was intrigued with what he learned from his kite string and key in 1752, but more than a century would pass before visionaries such as Michael Faraday and Edison could devise the next steps toward taming this strange natural energy.

Second, unlike bushels of wheat, bales of cotton, barrels of oil, or logs of wood, electric current cannot be visualized in tangible terms—who can actually take hold of a kilowatt-hour, even while paying for quite a few of them every month? Electricity is not a commodity to be stored in a warehouse for distribution to the marketplace on demand.

Except in very limited applications, such as flashlight, computer, and car batteries, electricity cannot be stored. Rather, it must be produced, "harvested," for dispatch to a consumer, who places an order by flipping a switch.

Electricity as delivered to modern societies is not a primary source of usable energy; it is called a carrier commodity. Typically, a primary commodity, such as coal, oil, gas, or uranium, must first be consumed to convert the fuel's nascent energy into useful electricity. The functional equivalent of a warehouse for the commodity of electricity, therefore, is the power plant. There electricity is "stored" not in bales or tanks but as the energy potential within a more manageable fuel. The primary commodity boils water to produce steam, to turn a turbine through a magnetic field. Out comes electricity.

Within that schematic picture, of course, lurk many layers of technology and policy. The destination for a power plant's output is not the home owner flipping a switch but a network of transmission lines and substations called "the grid." Scores, hundreds, of generating plants contribute their output to the grid, which in turn transmits electricity to thousands, millions, of consumers. Given the sophisticated grid structure that has evolved since the time of Thomas Edison and Samuel Insull, electricity customers generally are not dependent on the output of any one power plant; dozens of others kick in when needed. Decades of experience allow calculations of likely electricity demand through the seasons and at different times of day. Some power plants are relied on for a constant supply, called the "base load"; others contract to be available for "peak loads," during the early hours of twilight, for instance, when lights are turned on, or on the hottest days, when air conditioners drive up the demand.

Power plants are busy industrial facilities, but their control centers are deceptively placid. Two or three engineers lounge around in a windowless room, facing consoles of computer screens, buttons, and levers, twenty-four hours a day.

Over an eight-hour shift, nothing special may happen. Outside, supposing the plant's primary fuel to be coal, cargo ships tie up at the dock on schedule to unload their energy-rich cargo from, say, West Virginia or Indonesia for the coming week's work. Across from the control room, fires in the giant boilers, four or five stories high, burn in a gentle rumble to produce the steam that drives a sleek enclosed turbine in yet another nearby building.

In the United States (other countries have different standards), the turbines turn at 3,600 revolutions per minute, generating a steady flow of sixty-cycle alternating current. A contract between the power plant and the grid operators determines each plant's expected output, based on the estimate of what the grid's regional customers—residential, commercial, and industrial—will demand over the next minutes and hours.

That is the routine. The ability to adjust the operations of, for instance, a circulating fluidized-bed "clean coal" power plant from within this control room is only a mouse click away. A typical console will have buttons marked simply with up arrows and down arrows. Suppose the engineer on duty sees, on one of the real-time screens of consumer demand, that the grid is experiencing unexpected requests for more electricity, right now. The engineer can click on the up arrow to increase the plant's output to the hungry grid in its moment of need. Here is what happens:

- The first relay from the up arrow speeds up the conveyor belt carrying the coal from the pile outside into the bottom of the boilers; with more fuel, the boiler temperature rises.
- Simultaneously, another motor revs up to add more pebbles of limestone to the boiler, mixing with the burning coal to absorb sulfur dioxide, a noxious cause of acid rain and human respiratory ailments, released by the coal's combustion.
- Yet another motor speeds up, driving fans to push air into the boiler to encourage the higher combustion.
- As the burning ash gets hotter, so does the water piped through the boiler; more steam builds at the top.
- That requires more water to fill the tubes, so a motor driving the water pump adds to the flow.
- The newly building head of steam passes through the ducts to the turbine, spinning away at the constant speed required by the grid but against the higher pressure of more steam; resistance builds up in the generator; more electricity flows out to the transmission lines connecting the plant to the grid.

Within seconds of the click on the up arrow, sensors in the quiet control room show the progress of each of these steps. After two or three minutes, as the process moves through the system, the meter showing the electricity output of the plant moves up a few digits. Thus one power plant, presumably along with a dozen or even a hundred others linked to the regional grid, increases the supply of electricity to meet the immediate demand.

So much for the routine. Sometimes something unexpected happens; as in a home or an office during a power surge, a circuit breaker might trip—in this complex industrial plant there are dozens of them at every critical juncture. The signals on the consoles flash; red lights brighten every corner of the control room. A malfunction of one essential motor? A routine maintenance check by a worker who forgot to warn the control room in advance of his benign intervention? It might even be a glitch somewhere way off in the grid, having nothing to do with the operation of any one power plant. But since all the grid's turbines are tightly linked in their output, all plants are hit.

This sort of thing may happen only once or twice a year, but when it does, all the interconnected machinery in the plant stops. Conveyor belts grind to a halt. The head of steam at the top of the boilers is immediately released into the air, forming white clouds visible for a mile around; as the steam condenses, water showers from the overhead piping drench the plant's access driveways and sidewalks. The turbine winds down; no electricity flows out as plant engineers struggle to identify and repair the offense. Once the problem is identified and repaired, perhaps a few hours later, the routine of the power plant resumes.

Given the frighteningly volatile nature of the "merchandise" in these warehouses, power plants can be dangerous places. Hard hats and thick-soled shoes are mandatory at all times. Not a hand or foot must be set wrong; surveillance and vigilance are the rule, every moment of the day and night.

An electricity warehouse can surely be emptied and closed up like any other place where commodities are stored—that is called decommissioning a power plant—but as a practical matter it takes months, maybe years, to complete. As for building a new facility to meet anticipated demand, a nuclear plant for the traditional utility industry may require as much as ten years of lead time and, in the meantime, an enormous investment of capital and engineering resources.

Close to ten thousand power plants across the United States feed the nation's need for electricity. From California's Huntington Beach, renowned as "Surf City," to the East River waterfront abutting the United Nations headquarters in New York, to the Thames River in Connecticut, where Yale rowing crews train to beat Harvard every year, electric power plants have become ubiquitous on the horizon of the industrial world.

The reasonable goal of energy policy is not to deny the necessity of power plants in the community but rather to make them less troublesome to neighborhood sensitivities, more efficient in delivering the services that the community expects—and to mitigate the damage to the global environment that, over unthinking decades, they have caused.

While AES Deepwater was under construction, Sant and Bakke pursued prospects for other cogeneration plants with B. F. Goodrich Chemical, Gulf Oil, and the Occidental Chemical Corporation, none of which came to fruition. Once again, it was ARCO that came up with a challenge for entrepreneurship in the independent power industry.

Atlantic Richfield had acquired an old electricity plant attached to the company's chemical works near Pittsburgh. The installation, called Beaver Valley, had an illustrious past, a modest present, and, as far as ARCO could see, not much of a future at all. At the basic plant, built early in World War II, synthetic rubber had been developed with a secret process said to have been captured from Nazi Germany by American intelligence agents. Secured within massive, impenetrable concrete walls, Beaver Valley accomplished its strategic mission admirably. But after the war, as synthetic rubber developed a commercial life of its own, the old heap had to convert to inefficient use in the manufacture of chemicals, a rusty remnant of glory from an era gone by. Locals called it a sleeping giant.

ARCO kept four of Beaver Valley's coal-burning boilers working to produce steam and a trickle of electricity, a mere fraction of its wartime capacity, for backup use by the chemical plant. In the early 1980s, as the energy crisis transformed the world of Big Oil, ARCO's chemical division was ready to unload its unproductive power plant at Beaver Valley—if anyone would take it.

Deep in the ranks of ARCO Chemical Company was a plucky chemical engineer named Tom Tribone, who had been sent at company expense to business and law schools. In February 1982, the company handed Tribone the challenge of assessing whether some good could come out of Beaver Valley in the new economy of electric power. The head of ARCO Chemical, Hal Sorgenti, had come to know Sant at Deepwater as imaginative and adventurous; this might be just his thing.

Studying the old blueprints and operating reports for a presentation to Sant, Tribone was discouraged. As hard as he tried, he could not make the numbers add up to a profitable cogeneration enterprise. The costs of refitting the plant—efficiency and environmental standards had been of no concern during World War II—collided with the absence of likely long-term customers for either the electricity or the steam, at the modest levels assumed to be Beaver Valley's capacity.

About to give up, Tribone wandered through a darkened, unused section of the old plant, only to see looming above him a high black shadow that was not marked on his blueprints. "Oh, that's another boiler that we don't use anymore," the local engineer explained. If that forgotten boiler could be brought back online, it would add one-fifth more generation capacity to the four boilers kept in desultory operation. Suddenly all the numbers changed, very much for the better.

Retrofitting obsolescent coal-burning power plants was not exactly the Sant-Bakke vision for the energy future. All through 1983 and into 1984, they haggled with ARCO about the terms for taking over the albatross. At the same time, they looked for customers, Pennsylvania utilities ready to commit to buy the enlarged Beaver Valley output on long-term contracts, under the terms of PURPA. A tentative deal was finally struck in June 1984.

Between signing the letter of intent and turning the turbine, however, loomed a long road of obtaining the environmental permits necessary for retrofitting a power plant of a long-gone era, a process likely to consume two or three years' worth of engineering and legal effort. Like any good law student, Tribone ignored the conventional arguments for and against something new and went straight to the published regulations. There he found an obscure passage that, in effect, grandfathered power plants that had been in continuous operation so that the permitting need not take as long as it would for a new source. AES had included in its financial and engineering plans all the measures necessary to make the old coal-burning boilers acceptable under the new emission levels; now the securing of legal permits would not slow the project's gathering momentum.

Tribone recalled a telephone call from a friend in New England, a venture capital scout, the day after the Beaver Valley permits were announced. "When can I come down to see Mr. Sant's new power plant?" the eager caller asked. Never mind that "Mr. Sant's plant" did not exist, that the only thing to show was a decrepit old power station from World War II; the start-up company of Applied Energy Services was starting to attract attention from ever-widening, previously skeptical, financial circles.

AES completed the purchase of the Beaver Valley relic in August 1985, for $35 million; the company budgeted nearly three times that price for the retrofitting necessary to wake up the old sleeping giant to embark upon a long and useful new life.

The episode inspired Bakke to conjure a comic skit for presentation at AES orientation weekends for years to come, called "The Saga of Beaver Valley." Through a series of spoofing melodramas, company executives acted out horrendous ups and downs in negotiations to close a deal. "We would express great anger, and then we would agree," Bakke said. Everyone had fun remembering the ordeals, but the skit had a serious purpose in presenting to new employees a key element of the company culture: the important quality of tenacity that would come to characterize AES among insiders and outsiders alike during the coming decades of entrepreneurship and growth.

Sant summed up his financial strategy in talks with business students: "Our role was to forge compromise and creative solutions, and provide reassurance. We identify the 1 percent that is crucial to us in a project, and work very hard to make that happen. We can be very flexible on the other 99 percent."

"Mr. Sant" wanted a third cogeneration plant to establish operational credibility and stability for his company; he called it "the third leg of the stool."

Even as negotiations were engaged in for Deepwater and Beaver Valley, a further prospect came into view in the far West: a relatively small (100-megawatt) proposed plant to provide electric power in the Los Angeles area.

Located in an oil field in the Newhall industrial neighborhood, a backwater southeast of the city center, the new plant came to be called AES Placerita. Its distinctive features were, first, that it could be fueled by natural gas, plentiful in southern California. Second, the steam cogenerated would be put to one of those so-called exotic uses: it was to be pumped into the ground of the surrounding oil field for what was called tertiary recovery, forcing out oil that could not be accessed by conventional drilling. "The cost of recovering the oil from the Placerita fields should be less than half the normal cost," Sant and Bakke told investors. That was the theory.

AES had entered into a tentative partnership with the Tosco Oil Company, owner of the oil leases, in 1983, and had secured future sales contracts with Southern California Edison for the electricity and with Tosco itself for the steam output. But it would take three more years of tedious negotiation to arrange a relatively simple financing package for the $95 million project (the cost later rose to $112 million) and obtain the required environmental and land use permits.

Placerita was plagued with problems, starting with the sort of mechanical failure that the other AES plants had managed to avoid. On January 9, 1991, shortly after the start of commercial operation, the plant's steam turbine dropped a crucial blade, causing serious damage. Teams of technicians from all over AES converged to help the local crew assess the disaster. The repair effort took nearly five months, with additional downtime later in the year.

A more fundamental problem gradually emerged. Even with all the economical and sophisticated tertiary recovery techniques, oil production in the surrounding Tosco fields turned out to be a small fraction of what had been projected in the plant's financing package. Finally, in 1994, AES gave up on oil production at the Placerita venture.

Nonetheless, and despite all the mishaps lying ahead, Placerita became a third supporting stool leg, along with those in Texas and Pennsylvania, on which AES could stand as a growing independent power producer. In their annual report of 1985, Sant and Bakke indulged in an optimism that they firmly believed to be well grounded.

Looking three or four years ahead, when the first three "legs" would become fully operational, the founders projected their company's prospects. They calculated contracts already in place, covering electric revenues, steam revenues, and fuel costs, and factored in various assumptions that seemed reasonable. The results suggested sales of about $200 million, with after-tax profits of $7–$10 million, or $5.00–$7.15 per share. This was against an investment of $2.00 per share in 1982, for an unknown start-up in an untried new industry sector that just three years before had reported a per-share loss of $0.37.

FOUR

The Value of Values

In the early years of AES, Roger Sant and Dennis Bakke said little about what was in the back of their minds regarding the defining character of this unusual company engaged in the competitive business of generating electricity. AES' private prospectus of 1981 made no mention of ethical or social corporate values, nor did its first annual report of 1982 or the next four annual reports. "We never wrote it down in the early days," Sant acknowledged, insisting nonetheless that good corporate citizenship was as much an impetus for the founding of AES as was any new environmental technology or political deregulation.

In 1984, as the company approached its fourth year in operation, it set out to define a corporate culture during its annual summer retreat. At the time, the AES workforce numbered only in the dozens, and most of the staff could gather for a weekend together on Maryland's eastern shore. "We didn't know how strongly we felt about cultural things until we got into it," Sant later told his board of directors.

The notion of corporate social responsibility was not new. Samuel Insull, after all, had accepted a piece of it at the start of his enterprise building, early in the century, when he swore to an "obligation to serve" the public interest. In the mid-1920s, an upstart entrepreneur named Thomas J. Watson had startled the business community by injecting so-called people values into the heart of his new enterprise, which came to be called the International Business Machines Corporation—IBM.

Watson would deliver pep talks warning his executives against the "boss" mentality. In his unorthodox view, "a manager is an assistant to his men." IBM pioneered the radical concept of abolishing hourly wages in the manufacturing plants, seeking to eradicate subtle class distinctions by putting all employees on salary. Ever prodding workers to take responsibility for their actions, he decorated company offices with elegantly crafted little plaques bearing a single word, "THINK." (As the stern imperative spread outside the company, it became a target of office humor: " . . . OR THWIM" was a popular companion plaque—but only in offices far from the self-conscious culture of IBM.)

Watson's dedication to people values was no longer a topic for teasing by the 1970s. Autonomy and entrepreneurship at all levels had grown into a management theory; popular discussions of corporate governance such as *In Search of Excellence* by Thomas J. Peters and Robert H. Waterman Jr. became national best sellers. In the best-run companies, Peters and Waterman argued, "the good news comes from treating people decently and asking them to shine, and from producing things that work. Scale efficiencies give way to small units with turned-on people. . . . A numbing focus on cost gives way to an enhancing focus on quality. . . . Working according to fat rule books is replaced by everyone's contributing."

Sant and Waterman had met through their wives in California and had become good friends (Waterman later became a director of AES). In endless discussions with the Watermans, Sant was able to define working concepts that he had already found lacking in his own business career. Once established in Washington, DC, he found in Bakke a partner in fascination with the management of complex organizations. They both had found that bureaucratic hierarchies, in government and the private sector alike, stifled individual initiative and responsibility, Watson's imperative to THINK. Bakke shared Sant's eagerness for a new mode of management aimed at stimulating people to do their best work and actually enjoy their jobs. In odd moments they came to articulate, in the abstract, ideal corporate values for an enterprise that people would be proud to work for: social and community responsibility, not as charity but as integral to a profit-seeking corporation; an ethical imperative to "be fair" to everyone involved in corporate actions and decisions.

Sant insisted on something more. He ventured a word unusual in theories of corporate governance: "fun." This meant not just having a jolly good time on the job, certainly not the Friday afternoon beer busts of other progressive companies rediscovering the Watson style. Rather, to Sant, "fun" meant the sense of achievement and opportunity that every person involved, whatever the individual responsibilities, could anticipate every morning when coming to work, a sense of being in control of one's own labors, without artificial limits on anyone's potential contribution. As the AES culture took hold, the company tried to avoid such labels as "employees," "officers," and "workers." All were described as AES "people."

In later years, high-profile companies often paid lip service to Watson's people values without really putting them into practice. From the contemporary records of AES comes compelling evidence that the founders took their professed values very seriously indeed.

Discussion at the 1984 summer retreat, as Sant saw AES becoming "a real business," started on a concept called the "7-S Framework," devised by Waterman and Peters for McKinsey & Company. The point of this idea was to remind people that "organization" meant a lot more than structure. At a minimum, getting organized meant thinking about structure, strategy, systems, shared values, symbolic behavior, skills, and staff. The AES people later refined the McKinsey seven S's down to the AES four S's: shared values, super-ordinate goal, strategy, and a grab bag they called stuff. "Obviously, that's a stretch," Sant told his board of directors (inadvertently adding yet another "S"). "We didn't know what to call it. It's the characteristics of people at AES, the style, the behavior that you see around you."

Real-time articulation of Sant's vision of a corporate culture came in a 1985 memorandum he sent to his AES colleagues, by then numbering nearly eighty, after the retreat. Using the "Seven S's" was a statement of personal values, not prescriptive rules to follow whatever the context and circumstance. (The distinction became critical years later when AES was threatened with collapse and "It's the company culture" was offered as an excuse for poor performance.) Official company filings came to describe these values in the formal language required of a prominent public corporation. Long before that, Sant explained in his own musings the working philosophy he was setting out to make operational in "a real business."

Box 4.1

Memo to AES People From Roger Sant

Date: February 15, 1985

There should be little question as to how important I feel these cultural and strategic values are to the long-term success of the company. It is clearly not enough for us to be successful in a financial sense if the people—all of us—do not behave in a way that exemplifies these values. That is not to imply that these values are right and any others are wrong. It is simply my description of the way it will work best for us. . . .

Shared Values

Fun. We work because the work is fun, fulfilling and exciting, and when it stops being that way we will change what we do or how we do things.

Integrity. With customers and employees alike, we live with our agreements and statements, written or orally communicated, even if it hurts the company economically. Our commitment is sufficiently strong that our people and our customers can rely on our performance.

Fairness. We do not try to get the most out of a deal at the cost of being unfair to a customer or partner or related party. We believe in a basic ability to put ourselves in the other person's chair. We treat each other with respect and dignity. We treat customers as AES would want to be treated.

Social benefit. We want every project in which we are involved to, on the whole, make a positive contribution to society through lower cost to our customers, higher quality products, increased employment, cleaner environment or other similar benefits.

Strategy

New rules. Our business is to sell steam and electricity, . . . an old game but we're doing it under new rules. . . . We aspire to be the low-cost producer over the long term; favor capital intensive projects that can use low-cost project financing; create long term utility projects, not quick-kill deals; be the first to adopt newly commercial technologies; favor the use of design books and turnkey construction contracts. . . . We initiate rather than just react to projects conceived by others.

Symbolic Behavior

Openness and trust. We try not to hide concerns from each other. We demonstrate to our customers that we are capable and knowledgeable, but also that we do not have all the answers and have need for the input and help of others. We openly share information and our know-how and approach with our customers, contractors, vendors and bankers, and trust them to use that information responsibly.

Loyalty. We give the first opportunity for new positions to existing employees. Similarly we give the first opportunity for new financings, new projects, engineering/construction, consulting needs and other services to those with whom we have previously worked and enjoy ongoing relationships.

Exceptional performance. We are seldom satisfied as a team with anything but exceptional performance. We want to be the best at what we do.

Staff

Own the outcome. We encourage our people to be willing to do whatever it takes to get a job done—regardless of whose specific job assignment it is. We would like AES people to take responsibility without fear of punishment for accomplishing a task or project; not blame or make excuses because of organizational, people or other environmental factors.

Autonomous. We would like AES people to feel comfortable with—in fact, excited by—the autonomy they are given.

Developed from within. With few exceptions, the senior people of AES will develop from within the company and its culture; they will not be brought in from other organizations.

Skills

Cause action without power. Our strongest skill is to cause larger/more prestigious organizations to join us in completing projects. Thus we have a bias toward people who like to deal with complex relationships and personalities.

Adaptable. We would like our people to be adaptable, able to change to suit situations as they arise and able to learn new skills as those are required.

Systems

Support the AES culture. We want our systems to support our values, skills and staff—not let them "control." Our systems are guidelines, but always remaining flexible rather than rigid.

Structure

Decentralize. As AES grows, it is our intention to decentralize operations to the individual projects, to create entrepreneurial-type opportunities for people.

Sant and Bakke found themselves on the defensive as the collective impact of an unorthodox corporate value system began filtering out—to equity investors, new employees, even their own board of directors. "They are not statements of what we are; they are statements of what we would like to be," Sant told company meetings following that 1985 memorandum. "They are statements which give you the right to ask each of us, and each other, whether or not you thought that behavior was fair, or whether it had integrity, or whether it was responsible."

Against all challenges, a sense of humor survived within AES. On one of the S's, strategy, Roger Naill offered a straight-faced interjection at an orientation meeting for incoming employees: "I am in charge of strategic planning at AES. [Pause] AES does no strategic planning." Then Bakke would declare: "There are no corporate goals. No growth goals. No earnings targets. No central strategy. We try a bunch of stuff, we see what works, and we call that our strategy."

"It's almost a joke around AES," said Sant. "We call it ambiguity, but really it's chaos. We don't think things fit into neat little packages; we don't have organizational charts. We want to have people free to make the contributions they can make, and feel like they'd like to make." Or, as Waterman explained it, "If you see the problem, it's yours. You take the initiative to solve it"— whether it's in the boiler room or the parking lot, never mind your particular job or place in the organization.

Dutifully refined and spruced up, the management philosophy teased out of Sant's memo of 1985 was finally proclaimed to the company's small band of private investors in the annual report of 1987.

Readers of official corporate filings expect to learn financial results, and AES was never reticent about that. But many such readers must have been startled in 1987 to find the official report opening with a lengthy statement of corporate operating principles, a statement that AES used as a litany to define itself for years to come:

> These values play the central role in guiding how we approach our business:
>
> *Integrity*. We want our actions marked by integrity or "wholeness" where all that we do and say in all parts of the company fit together with truth and consistency. When one of us commits to some course of action verbally or in writing, we want that person and the rest of the organization to carry out the commitment regardless of its effect on the company's economic performance.

Bakke would tell skeptics that "integrity" means that "what we do matches what we say, matching talk with actions"—whether or not they enhance the bottom line.

Fairness. Our desire is that AES treat fairly its people, its customers, its suppliers, its shareholders, the communities in which it resides and all others indirectly affected by AES activities. Defining what is fair is often subject to considerable discussion. At the very least we want the question "Is it fair?" raised in the discussion of every important issue. We do not think it right to get the most out of each deal to the detriment of others, and we believe it is essential to put ourselves in the other person's position.

"The most important thing is just asking ourselves the question, 'Was what we did fair?'" Sant would explain. "Sometimes we'll get differing answers about that, but at least we have the right to ask each other."

Waterman recalled a banker visiting AES' Arlington headquarters in those early years and shaking his head. "I went by an office and two VPs were arguing about whether something was 'fair' or not. Can you *believe* that?" Naill said that being fair "sure makes for some fascinating sets of negotiations."

Fun. We want our people and those with whom the company interacts to have fun in their work. Our goal is to create and maintain an environment where each of us can flourish in the use of our gifts and skills and thereby have great enjoyment in the way we spend our time at AES.

This is the company value that caused AES the most trouble with the skeptics. "Fun is when you are intellectually excited and you are interacting with each other—one idea leading to another—and you're getting frustrated because there isn't an answer," said Sant, eyes flashing. "You work and you struggle and it's great when a plan comes together! It's the struggle, and even the failures that go with it, that makes it fun."

In endless discussions, he met all the predictable complaints head-on. "They say the purpose of being in a company is not to have fun, it's to do work. We wanted to put 'fun' in because we felt so strongly that that's not so. We do what we do, not because it's just a job, because we have to make a living, but because it's something we really enjoy doing. It's fulfilling, it's enjoyable, we like each other, we like what we do, and we're proud of what we do, so it's fun." Naill offered a terse summation: "If you dread coming to work every day, then we're doing something wrong."

> *Social Responsibility.* We feel a responsibility to be involved in projects that provide social benefits such as lower costs to our customers, a high degree of safety and reliability, increased employment, use of the best available environmental controls and a nurturing working environment.

In the budgets of new power plants around the world, from Oklahoma to Pakistan, were commitments accumulating to millions of dollars for local school systems, for instance. "This kind of gift and participation comes out of our philosophy," Bakke declared. "We want to do something extra to try to help meet the society's needs."

The extraordinary statement of operating values leading the AES annual report of 1987 concluded with an in-your-face message to the company's shareholders, banks, pension funds, and other hardy investors (AES was not yet publicly traded):

> You may have noted the absence of profits and shareholder wealth maximization from the statement of values. We believe profits are important. They are, however, not the goal of our enterprise. Rather, they are the likely and necessary results in a company that provides a quality product or *service.* . . . AES is seeking to be a clean, reliable, low-cost supplier of electricity and other energy. The shared values form the principles that guide our efforts toward that end.
>
> Hence, while earnings will be a measure that helps track AES performance, we want the values to guide how we *do* the business.

This may have seemed facile talk for an audacious start-up enterprise in a disruptive new industry. But, in fact, the history of AES as it matured would be one of testing, of examining how these declared operating principles would actually work out in a frenetic marketplace.

The irony in this story is that the values proclaimed by AES starting in 1985 became a theme song for much of the emerging independent power industry, as if virtue were somehow inherent in the deregulated generation of electricity. Competitors and partners alike professed to operate on ethical and social principles—until the financial meltdown of 2001, when bankruptcies, indictments, and convictions revealed cynical manipulations to the contrary.

From the years when AES was defining its identity, Naill recalled an early planning session. A cheerful new employee piped up, "Hey, these values are great. People like them. It's a great marketing ploy." Around him were people who had known Roger Sant from the start, and the room suddenly hushed. Sant broke the silence with a quiet anger rarely displayed, an intensity evident even to the new man. "I don't care whether it's a good marketing ploy or not. I want to try to live by these values because that is the way I think we ought to be. The day the company gives them up, I won't belong."

As the AES workforce grew into the thousands at power plants around the world, the founders considered it essential that the values Sant had started to articulate in 1985 be conveyed from a group of project developers and managers to the staff who actually operated the far-flung plants. Stepping forward to take on this task was Dave McMillen, plant manager at AES Deepwater. From a background of traditional, hierarchical chemical plant management, McMillen grew into the most enthusiastic and effective advocate of AES' values that the founders could ever have imagined.

AES had always granted equity shares in the company to its employees as part of the compensation package. By 1991, the growing number of AES shareholders threatened to exceed the limit of 500 for a privately held company. In a typical start-up company, where enrichment of the founding generation loomed large as a goal, the prospect of an initial public offering provoked pleasure measured in dollar signs. But at AES, "we faced the prospect with fear and trembling," Sant and Bakke informed their loyal cadre of stockholders in one internal report:

> Could we maintain our values and make decisions accordingly in the face of numerous new shareholders with a broader mix of objectives and expectations? Would we be forced to be different as a public company when clearly

we didn't want to be? Would our senior leadership people be required to
spend substantially more time involved in activities related to being a public corporation that took time away from other potentially more productive
activities?

Before deciding on a tender to the public and entering into negotiations with
financial attorneys, the two founders sent a reassuring memo to the entire
company:

> We continue to be committed to the purpose and values of AES, whether we
> continue as a private company or become a public corporation. If we find
> ourselves tempted to change any significant elements of the way we do busi-
> ness, we must consider that change to be a major red flag, and we should
> make the change only if our current rationale for acting as we do doesn't
> make sense—independent of the public offering process.

A prospectus offering shares to the public requires a formal description of the
company, but before that it requires an extravagant depiction of the risk factors in the proffered investment. When the U.S. Securities and Exchange
Commission saw how AES described itself, its values, and its attitudes toward
profit, the agency ordered this strange applicant to move the relevant para-
graphs out of the company description and into the section on risk factors.
When AES stock was offered to the public in 1991 for the first time, the
prospectus stated:

> *Adherence to AES's Values—Possible Impact on Results of Operations.* An important
> element of AES is its commitment to four major "shared" values: to act with
> integrity, to be fair, to have fun and to be socially responsible. . . . AES
> believes that earning a fair profit is an important result of providing a qual-
> ity product to its customers. However, if the Company perceives a conflict
> between these values and profits, the Company will try to adhere to its val-
> ues—even though doing so might result in diminished profits or foregone
> opportunities. Moreover, the Company seeks to adhere to these values not

as a means to achieve economic success, but because adherence is a worth-while goal in and of itself.

And there was more. Just in case the risk of investing in AES was not absolutely clear by this point, the prospectus put potential investors on notice with a final stern advisory: "The Company intends to continue these policies after this offering."

Waterman reported overhearing a salesman for the underwriters, who was preparing to offer AES stock to his customers, commenting, "Boy, that's pretty funny—our government's saying it's risky to try to do business by relying on fairness and integrity."

AES completed an initial public offering in June 1991 of about 10 percent of outstanding common stock in newly issued shares at $19.00, on reported earnings of $1.02 per share. (Adjusted for subsequent splits and stock dividends over the coming decade, the offering share price amounted to just over $3.00.)

If IBM's Thomas J. Watson is remembered as the prototype of the executive determined to inject human values into a business corporation, those who came later better appreciated the difficult and subtle techniques for employing those values in daily practice. Two young McKinsey partners, Julien Phillips and Allan Kennedy, argued that having a charismatic personality at the top is not enough. Rather, they wrote in a research paper, success in the effort derives "from obvious, sincere, sustained personal commitment to the values the leaders sought to implant, coupled with extraordinary persistence in reinforcing those values."

The enthusiasts coalescing around AES took this admonition to heart. Executives and officers spent a week every year on the floor of the power plants, decked out in overalls and hard hats, crawling through the machinery with the maintenance men to learn how they did their jobs and, more important, to learn their attitudes toward their work.

Waterman tells of Bob Hemphill visiting the old plant at Beaver Valley and being puzzled by some cumbersome operation left over from the former management. "Why do we do it like this?" he asked. The reply was, "They make us." Hemphill had no reply; on returning to headquarters, he swung into action. He dispatched to every AES employee a ceramic coffee mug emblazoned with the words, "Who Is They Anyway?" Then followed big posters of Sant in his office with the name plate on his desk "NOT THEY." Suggestion boxes spread through the company, inviting employees to "Send They a Letter." The climax of his campaign came at the next orientation meeting. Into the proceedings suddenly stormed four strangers in combat gear, brandishing fake rifles, with patches on their fatigues proclaiming the "Anti-They Liberation Front." The "guerrillas" were quickly overpowered and unmasked, revealing Bob Hemphill, Ken Woodcock, and the two men's wives.

When Bakke did his first executive workweek at Deepwater, he sat in while the plant's worker policy committee discussed a personnel issue that had just come up—how much time off should be granted when there is a death in the family. He listened in amazement and frustration as the workers deliberated the complications: What if the parent's funeral were overseas? What if the "parent" who died was not a biological parent but an uncle or aunt or a foster parent? This sort of thing flew straight against "stuff," the dignity of the individual. Bakke finally spoke up, asking why the company should not eliminate personnel manuals and all officious procedures and let workers themselves decide, whenever something came up, on the fair course of action for their colleague.

Nervously, the Deepwater team decided to give it a try. A short time later, an employee's mother was hospitalized and needed large amounts of blood for transfusion. This was an occasion for a human resources staff to take sympathetic action—but there was no human resources staff. Without announcements, word got around on the floor of the plant and, one by one, about three-quarters of Deepwater's employees went off on their own to the blood bank.

From the earliest years, both at the AES corporate headquarters in Arlington and in the power plants themselves, there were no personnel departments; no safety, environmental, or engineering divisions; and certainly no lobbying or public relations offices. Any decisions important to company strategy or values, Bakke argued, should not be controlled by separate departments; everyone who confronted the issue should have a say in resolving it. That was the meaning of "ownership."

Shunning ladders of hierarchy, AES called its organizational style a "honeycomb," with each worker relating not only upward and downward but also with others all around. Bob Price, who rose in the ranks under Dave McMillen's influence to become manager of a pioneering AES plant in Connecticut, summarized the company culture as it played out: no employee handbooks, manuals, or rules (except regarding safety); no operating, maintenance, or technical departments; no shift or maintenance supervisors; no specialized staff; no "turf." Every employee knew, and was accorded, responsibility.

One hard-hat worker spotted a subcontractor flouting safety procedures, and in a serious way. The AES man did not report the matter, nor did he seek anyone's permission to do something about it. He simply escorted the offending subcontractor to the gate of the power plant and dismissed him. When they heard about it, the plant manager and the officers in Arlington were proud of the worker's actions.

Personal responsibility became "part of our culture," McMillen declared in his regular pep talks to the work crews. "Personal responsibility means to your neighbors, to the air, to the water, to all the kinds of things that matter, whether it's noise or emissions. We think that the people who are hands-on at the plant level should be doing this kind of thing because, after all, it's their responsibility, they can control it—not some staffer at the corporate level."

With Sant at the helm as AES grew in recognition, Bakke fell into the role of chief operating officer. But he also assumed the role of public evangelist; even to financial analysts serving investors and lenders, he argued for corporate values over the more familiar goal of maximizing shareholder value. "Where do profits fit in?" he would ask. "Without turning a profit, a corporation, too, will cease to exist. At AES we strive not to make profits the ultimate driver of the corporation; the principles to which we strive take precedence."

Sant and Bakke had not grown up in the rough and dangerous business of generating electricity. What they had done, starting from an impulse, was create a company they wanted to work for—and if it would make profits, "breathe," that would make it sustainable.

A maintenance man at one AES power plant told a visitor three things about his job:

1. "You'll look over your shoulder to ask permission, and there's nobody there."
2. "I feel free to admit it honestly if I screw up."
3. "You know what's really unusual about this place? Everybody shakes hands when they report to work."

FIVE

Plants and Trees

The means for generating electricity had registered major progress by the 1980s. New technologies were there for the taking, with agreeable profitability, in new "greenfield" power plants, built from the ground up. But America's power infrastructure was weighed down by a mighty inventory of obsolescent power plants built thirty or forty years before and still operating as they always had—burning dirty fuels inefficiently with primitive technologies, and comfortably grandfathered under the federal Clean Air Act.

Typical utility managers calculated that the expense of retrofitting the old plants to meet new standards of efficiency and environmental protection would not be accompanied by acceptable returns, so they continued to rely on the plants' protected status. The largely depreciated capital investments of earlier coupon-cutting years, after all, were still generating respectable profits.

Hungry upstarts at AES and the other deregulated power companies pressed their argument that modern technologies could make a new power plant more than twenty times cleaner than one built just ten or fifteen years before. And the economic and social benefits would kick in the day a new plant started operation because its output would replace the electricity generated under the dirty conditions acceptable in an earlier era.

The 1970s energy reformers relished the vision of a system of small neighborhood power plants, like those of Edison's Pearl Street, where intrusive high-voltage transmission lines would not have to carry the current from generator to consumer. But even if the economies of scale that justified large central power stations had run out, those economies did not totally disappear. In the economics of electricity, small cannot always be beautiful. A certain size is necessary to spread out the costs of engineering, efficiency, and environmental control technologies. A web of mini power plants, or "distributed power," as it is now called, seemed enticing to New Age theorists, but except for a few special cases, on their own they could not support the mandated cleanup costs (if they burned fossil fuels) or the research and development investments required to make renewable energy sources practical. And this vision for a new era would only multiply the number of industrial power plants marring the landscape.

The start-ups of the independent power sector found an optimum size for new plants at about 200 megawatts, more or less, depending on the setting. But this meant that for every obsolete central power station decommissioned, two or three smaller ones would have to be built. Ever more unwieldy Erector sets would have to show up in the nation's backyards, and neighborhood resistance became one factor that the early visionaries had not fully appreciated.

Once established on the three legs of the AES stool, having built innovative power plants in Texas, Pennsylvania, and California, Roger Sant and Dennis Bakke sat back to indulge in some long-term projections for a revised business plan. Their conclusions, necessarily theoretical, were nonetheless startling.

Simple analysis began on the assumption that demand for electricity would continue growing at the rate of the 1980s. Second came an assumption that the legal, technological, and economic incentives already in place would be enough to induce established utilities to replace outdated and dirty generating plants still in operation. Given these conditions, the number crunching reached a numbing conclusion: to meet the expected demand with state-of-the-art technology, one new 200-megawatt power plant would have to go online in the United States *every five days!*

Catching their breath, Sant, Bakke, and Roger Naill sought greater clarity, and prudence, by refining their assumptions and data more carefully. Perhaps the growth rate in demand for electricity over the recent past need not be carried into the future. After all, their campaigns in government and academia had argued that conservation of energy would significantly lower demand. If the least-cost energy strategy, or something like it, were to take hold, what would be a reasonable reduction in future demand?

Into the AES database in Arlington they fed broader and more refined data: impacts on aggregate demand of growing energy productivity, factoring in population growth; realistic estimates of retrofitting opportunities for operators of old plants, even when strong incentives were lacking. Clicking onto the bottom line of their revised spreadsheets, they found that in the United States alone, one new 200-megawatt plant would be needed (only) every fifteen days—a couple dozen every year.

These numbers, of course, were abstractions built on assumptions drawn from generalizations. The analysis blurred the reality that demand for electricity would not necessarily grow consistently in a straight line, and, more crucially, it overlooked the ingenuity of entrenched utilities in keeping their old behemoths in operation long after considerations of efficiency and clean technologies demanded that they be scrapped.

Nonetheless, AES and its competitors in the deregulated power-producing sector found enough of the confirmation they needed: theirs was a spectacular growth industry. The wave of a disruptive transformation was building; all the hungry newcomers needed to do was catch it.

What would their state-of-the-art new power plants look like? Where would they be sited—accessible to fuel and to long-term customers for both electricity and, given the statutory requirement of the cogeneration principle, steam? Would neighboring communities allow industrial facilities to be placed in their backyards? Technology and beautification could go only so far.

Most acutely, what primary commodity would the new plants consume in order to heat the water into steam to turn the turbine? In the visions of the environmentally conscious 1970s and beyond, renewable fuels would come along to generate the nation's electricity: solar power, wind power, all the so-called exotic alternatives to the familiar fossil fuels, which energy and utility industries had taken for granted, and on which they had grown quite comfortable.

Sant and his fellow entrepreneurs at AES shared the reforming zeal of environmentalists, but their working focus was on private-sector efforts to conserve energy and use it more efficiently, not on the scientific quest for renewable energy sources. "A totally renewable or non–fossil fuel mix" remained the desired long-term pursuit, AES declared after its first decade in operation. But in the coming few years, for a business aiming to serve the demand for energy services, the fuels of choice could be only the familiar ones, suitably cleaned up to minimize environmental damage.

During these years AES never considered building nuclear power plants; environmental and public security concerns aside, nuclear technologies required plants of massive size and a capital investment that could not be raised in private markets. Given this burdensome capital load, the cost per unit of nuclear-generated electricity at that time did not even come close to competing. The economically viable alternatives, as AES designed its new business plan, remained oil, natural gas, and coal.

To the dismay of many of their energy reforming colleagues, Sant and Bakke settled on coal as their fuel of choice for new AES power plants. "Coal is not the *only* answer," they hastened to declare in their 1990 annual report, "but it is an essential *part* of the solution for the time being."

For a thousand years, the dynasties of China had burned coal in their blast furnaces. It was coal, in massive amounts, that had fired the Industrial Revolution. "This fossil fuel became synonymous with wealth and modernity in the 19th century," wrote Seth Dunn of the Worldwatch Institute, an environmentally concerned research center that Sant had long supported. A widely heeded Victorian economist, William Jevons, had warned in a classic 1865 study that the British Empire would collapse as its coal mines approached depletion.

Not that anyone paid much attention back then, but coal was about the most polluting, most noxious commodity known to the industrial world, beginning with its extraction from the earth and continuing all the way to its consumption in the boilers of the power plants. Strip mines destroyed land-scapes; extraction from rich veins deep under the surface took a terrible toll on generations of miners. During extraction and transit, coal dust (particulates) appeared as soot, dirtying the air and the lungs of people who breathed it. Firing to release the coal's energy also released huge quantities of sulfur dioxide and nitrogen oxides into the sky, where they either combined with other chemicals, creating acids that fell back to the earth in rain, snow, fog, and smog, or turned into acid on direct contact, causing corrosion on buildings and other structures and damage to vegetation, rivers, and lakes.

The Clean Air Act and its amendments in the 1970s aimed to change that. The act established quantitative levels for acceptable emissions of the known pollutants from new power plants. It led to so-called clean coal technology, which succeeded in addressing the main types of pollution that had continued unchecked for centuries. Sant, prophet of the least-cost energy strategy, argued that coal firing was the most cost-efficient means of producing electricity, even when the expense of environmental cleanup was factored in. New coal-fired power plants averaged about one-tenth the noxious emissions of the old utility plants. "Technology has all but eliminated coal pollution as society has traditionally measured it," Sant told skeptical academic conferences. (The inadequacy of the "traditional measurements" was not yet clearly perceived.) For a century to come, he argued, coal would be "an abundant worldwide fuel source, so prices will not rise because of threatened shortages or political disruptions."

The AES zealots pressed their case with disillusioned environmentalist critics. Coal offered a way out of dependence on insecure foreign oil sources: "A 300-megawatt AES coal plant saves 170 million gallons of imported oil per year," Bakke argued, to say nothing of the foreign policy and defense resources engaged in protecting access to overseas reserves. The benefits to the national and local economies went on and on, in the AES presentation: a power industry fueled by coal created three or four times the number of jobs, in all related sectors, as did comparably sized natural gas or oil-burning plants. Because they cost more to build, coal-burning power plants were assessed double or even triple the local taxes of a natural gas facility producing the same amount of electricity. Tangible benefits to an entire community, AES argued, could become a significant trade-off for a power plant's impact on the backyards of a few.

In sum, Sant and Bakke committed their company to the use of coal in pursuing the least-cost energy strategy in a socially responsible way: beneficial to the communities where the electricity would be generated, fair to the customers who would buy it at the lower costs allowed by technology, unencumbered by huge capital investments. They were determined and confident, moreover, that they could do the job within all the restraints—mandated and anticipated—of honest environmental protection.

Notably absent in those early decisions was consideration of the fact that the environmental damage from burning coal did not stop with emissions of sulfur dioxide and nitrogen oxides, the traditional pollutants addressed by federal regulations, which made the air around a power plant dangerous to breathe. As environmental science grew more sophisticated, it became clear that coal-burning power plants also release into the atmosphere carbon dioxide (CO_2), one of the most ominous of the greenhouse gases that threaten climate change worldwide. "Coal releases 29 percent more carbon per unit of energy than oil," according to Worldwatch, "and 80 percent more than natural gas."

This posed no particular danger to the backyards, but cumulatively it affected the health of the entire globe. Having resolved to their satisfaction the known local environmental injuries of their operations, Sant and his AES power plants soon had to confront an offense far more threatening.

As the databases in Arlington churned out their projections, Ken Woodcock, the mechanical engineer turned air pollution expert, found an outlet for his expertise more appropriate than his first AES job of running a computer in the corridor. His assignment was to scout out sites around the country where AES might do its share in building the dozens of new electricity plants necessary to power the nation's future.

Cogeneration was the mandate of the law, so the first criterion in site selection was a nearby customer for the steam once it had done its work driving the plant's turbines. Electric current can be dispatched over longer distances than steam, so the location of the electricity customers came second.

Then of crucial importance was ready access to fuel supplies to fire the boilers. A fuel supplied in bulk, such as coal or oil, required a plant site with a good deepwater or rail connection. Finally, since a power plant can be a sprawling installation, the site had to provide space for all the attendant facilities—and in a setting of minimal disturbance to the neighborhood.

In the course of their consulting work, Roger Naill and his analysts were ever on the alert for suitable sites and potential customers for electricity and steam. Woodcock, roaming the country by car, plane, and helicopter, evaluated a dozen or more possible locations at a time. In December 1984, he spotted a promising setting in eastern Connecticut. There a modest old paperboard factory had just been acquired by the Stone Container Corporation, a large enterprise experienced in a steam-intensive business.

On a whim over the New Year's break, Woodcock drove over from Rhode Island, where he was vacationing with his family, to look for the community of Uncasville, stopping at every cluster of industrial buildings that might be a paperboard factory on the River Thames. (Despite what they call it in England, the name of the river in Connecticut rhymes with "games.") When he found the place, he decided it was worth a more formal return visit.

The new paper plant manager saw obvious value in a source of cheap steam but took the precaution of sending Woodcock over to the first selectman of Uncasville (in effect, the mayor) to test the local political mood. AES representatives outlined their $260 million proposition over the coming weeks, taking care to detail the tax revenues and jobs that a new power plant would provide for the community. Woodcock recalled a town elder handing over a thick sheaf of environmental and building regulations, saying, "If you folks can make your way through all this, you won't have any trouble with us."

Community support from the outset had proved crucial in such enterprises. In the long buildup to construction of the Placerita plant in southern California, AES executives had found that nothing was accomplished in big, angry meetings where neighbors outdid one another in dire warnings about an intruding power plant. "So we started going door-to-door to talk to everyone individually," said Bob Hemphill. "We visited 120 homes. We'd usually spend a half hour to an hour, but sometimes we stayed for five or six hours—

as long as it took to answer their questions." (In years to come, AES planners occasionally grew careless about heeding this experience and confronted less than friendly welcomes for future ventures.)

Uncasville met almost all the criteria needed by an independent power producer: docking access for coastal cargo ships delivering weekly consignments of West Virginia coal from the port of Baltimore; an industrial steam customer next door; an established electric utility in the area with a rich customer base across eastern Connecticut, obligated under the terms of the PURPA statute to buy, at a price attractive to the producer, electricity offered to the grid. Only the size of Stone Container's riverside plot gave pause: no more than seven acres would be available, closely abutting a settled residential neighborhood. This site, a fraction of what a power plant would normally require, called for ingenuity in engineering and construction. Access roads, river cooling, smokestack emissions, and output cabling could not be allowed to disrupt Uncasville's small single-family homes and waterfront paths.

At its first three plants, which settled AES in the business of cogenerating electricity, the company had focused on the steam customer's needs. On the Thames, AES could demonstrate what it called its new "independent" strategy and emphasize the electricity; the fledgling company chose to make this plant a model for a responsible role in America's electricity future. To make good on the company's commitment to coal as its fuel of choice, the AES Thames plant would pioneer a new "clean coal" technology called circulating fluidized-bed boilers.

By 1985, as serious planning for the Thames plant got under way, Sant and Bakke and their executives had learned some of the cruel lessons of assembling financing packages. "It's like picking up a puddle of mercury with your hands," Woodcock said. "Some bit of it is always going to fall out somewhere." Negotiations over the next year or so involved no fewer than twenty-seven participating financial institutions and fourteen law firms. The finances and liquidity of AES, to say nothing of the mental well-being of the company officers, were stressed close to the limit.

AES Thames entered into commercial operation in March 1990, and ever since then it has supplied a minimum of 181 megawatts of electricity twenty-four hours a day, 365 days a year: enough power for 100,000 homes. With cogeneration, steam pours out at 25,000 to 100,000 pounds per hour, enabling Stone Container to recycle 155,000 tons of corrugated cardboard every year.

Operating efficiency exceeded the most optimistic expectations for a modern power plant. The relevant measure is "availability," the percentage of online capacity that a plant actually uses to deliver power over a year; against an industry average of 83 percent, AES Thames has consistently operated at 95 percent.

As AES strategists intended, the Thames design became the model for plants to come, in Oklahoma, Hawaii, and beyond. More than a hundred engineers and technicians who learned the trade at Thames fanned out with their operating and managerial experience to AES power plants around the world. Of the first twenty-four people hired to run AES Thames, Bakke calculated, two became corporate vice presidents, eight became plant managers, and seven went on to lead business development teams. "And they're all generalists; they know most aspects of our operations inside and out."

As for emissions of sulfur dioxide, nitrogen oxides, and particulates, the pollutants regulated by the Clean Air Act, the AES coal-fired plants operating on the Thames model consistently record results far below the levels that federal, state, and local regulators deem acceptable, both those currently in place and proposed.

There remained the problem of carbon dioxide. The phenomena of global warming and climate change were only beginning to imprint themselves on the public mind in the late 1980s as clean coal plants such as AES Thames were in design and construction. Futurists of the era, such as Sant's early soul mate in energy reform, Amory Lovins, began to warn that the major share of CO_2 in the atmosphere arose from the burning of fossil fuels—and that fully one-third of the ominous greenhouse gases were emitted by fossil-fuel-burning electric power plants.

By this time, Sant had joined the board of directors of the World Resources Institute (WRI), an environmental think tank. After long briefings from WRI analysts, he ruefully acknowledged that his vaunted "clean coal" had not addressed CO_2 emissions. Even though it was not a legal requirement, he decided that his company's operations would somehow have to confront the looming problem of global warming. The new AES plant on the Thames, with no inherited infrastructure to contend with, could from the start build in a cost factor to mitigate that modest share of the threatened global warming that one new power plant would contribute.

Pursuing the management philosophy of steering the talents of workers toward projects that excited them, Sant assigned the task of researching ways to offset greenhouse gas emissions to employee number five, Sheryl Sturges.

Sturges had grown weary of defending the AES coal strategy to her ecology-minded father and husband; grudgingly she had accepted the decision in terms of business economics and national security. She had no trouble showing that clean coal technologies worked for the traditional air pollutants. But then came the matter of CO_2 and global warming. "We got our hands on everything we could read, at the Library of Congress and the Yale School of Forestry, for starters," she said in an interview. "The first avenue we pursued was technology." Unfortunately, all the scrubbers and mechanical devices designed to deal directly with the problem not only were unreasonably expensive but also had environmentally destructive side effects.

Schoolchildren have long been taught that human beings inhale oxygen and exhale carbon dioxide, while the opposite happens with green trees and foliage, which "inhale" carbon dioxide, keep the carbon for themselves, and "exhale" the oxygen. This, the process of photosynthesis, was nature's way of sustaining ecological balance between people and vegetation. Such a fundamental fact seemed too simpleminded and obvious to be taken seriously in the new discipline of environmental science.

The moment came when Sant asked Sturges to deliver a report. "I'm sure Roger was thinking I was going to propose fertilizer production or fuel cells, and here I was saying 'plant trees,'" Sturges recalled. "I thought the operating committee would think I was crazy; it was a crazy idea—no one, not even my own ecologist father, had ever heard of doing it."

Sturges had quickly grown beyond simplistic notions of just planting trees all around the Thames power station, even if there had been enough room on the constricted plot. The danger of greenhouse gases occurs high in the atmosphere, not in the air immediately around the emitting source. That is why CO_2 did not figure in the Clean Air Act regulations.

Carbon-absorbing trees almost anywhere in the world would serve the purpose. "The winds of the world kind of mix everything up in less than three weeks," reasoned the Thames plant manager, Dave McMillen, as he caught on to the idea, "so if you plant trees in some part of the world where they grow real fast, then these trees can help take the CO_2 out of the air."

Sturges and Sant had stumbled on a true innovation, but the idea did not stop there. Any program to enlarge and sustain forest cover in regions of rampant poverty would serve broader goals of raising a poor population's living standards as well as absorb offending emissions from industrial power stations. Accordingly, AES solicited proposals from economic development agencies and opted to join forces with CARE, one of the largest nongovernmental development aid organizations. CARE had been operating a project in Guatemala, combining agriculture and forestry, since 1974.

In the science of agroforestry, trees are planted strategically: to enhance and complement crop growth, for instance; in rows as windbreaks to reduce soil erosion or on the contours of steep terrain to prevent soil from washing downhill; as fencing to protect crops from marauding animals. CARE had practical expertise in these techniques. But AES' interest presented the agroforestry specialists with a new challenge: "We have never before seriously considered the impact of our projects in terms of carbon fixation," the aid agency admitted. "Preparation of this proposal has been a learning experience for CARE."

The planners of the Thames plant were prepared to include in their budget a long-term commitment of $2 million for a carbon offset project, a sum just about equal to AES' entire profits for 1989. To create accountability, they asked WRI to calculate how many trees would be needed to absorb the carbon emitted over the plant's expected forty-year life span. Using only the crudest hypothetical model and with no field experience to back them up, the WRI analysts suggested that 52 million trees would do the trick, a statistic that sounded precise but blurred so many of the variables as to be little more than a rough guideline.

When AES announced the program, critics seized upon the artificial number of 52 million, not the more meaningful refinements: efficient fire brigades to protect growing trees from forest fires; land use training to help indigenous farmers be more productive; a halt to traditional and ruinous deforestation—such measures served the goal of absorbing tons of carbon over decades at least as well as did planting seedlings.

In pioneering a novel program to offset carbon emissions, AES had become the butt of parody. Sturges treasured on her refrigerator door at home a *New Yorker* cartoon portraying a befeathered witch doctor receiving a team of "suits" from the city and divining some magic number of trees to propitiate for their nefarious industrial enterprise. To Sant's annoyance over the years, mining companies seized upon the AES initiative as a public relations bonanza for the coal industry. A *New York Times* writer remarked: "There are so many parrots and jungle scenes in [a coal company's] corporate literature that you'd think the company was headquartered on the banks of the Amazon."

Within the culture of AES, the Thames initiative caught on and became a standard fixture in the budgeting for future power plants. The company's 180-megawatt cogeneration plant on the island of Oahu, AES Barbers Point, which opened in 1992, committed funding to preserve a forest in Paraguay nearly two and one-half times the area of Washington, DC, protecting it from threatened deforestation through commercial logging and conversion to agriculture and thus sustaining its capacity to absorb atmospheric carbon. The AES Shady Point power plant in Oklahoma, a larger, 320-megawatt clone of AES Thames, joined forces with Oxfam International and representatives of indigenous peoples in Peru, Ecuador, and Bolivia to protect 1.2 million acres of tropical rain forest at a cost of $3 million.

Sant was proud of his company's initiative. "It met our own concern head-on," he said. "We actually take more CO_2 out of the atmosphere than we put in. It also produced a direct link for our operating people within a very emotional field—the environment. We established a very simple environmental quid pro quo."

Carbon dioxide from power plants burning fossil fuels may be the major single source of contamination in the atmosphere, but it is not the only culprit in global warming. In second place is methane. What on earth is methane, and how is it released into the stratosphere? Textbooks explain that methane is the largest component of natural gas, it builds up in coal mines, and it is a product of decomposition of vegetable matter under water—it is sometimes called marsh gas.

Sant, Sturges, and the ecologists knew all this. But they also knew a little more, which they found embarrassing to discuss outside the circles of environmental scientists. The most widespread natural source of the methane rising high above Earth is the world's population of livestock; it is a large part of the gas passed by cattle in the course of their digestion. When Sturges cautiously explained this part of the research, Bakke, for one, understood exactly what she was talking about; he knew a good deal about the smell of cows from his own farm boyhood.

Livestock experts had found that a modest injection of molasses into normal cattle feed would dramatically reduce the methane emitted, and the consequent corruption of the stratosphere, without inhibiting the cows' digestive comfort.

If AES had become the butt of jokes by planting trees, think of the derision that would befall the company's interest in reducing the flatulence of cows. These natural methane emissions had nothing directly to do with coal-burning power plants, but AES decided that if they contributed to global warming, the company would do something about the problem. Alongside a new power plant in India in 1994 and another that followed in Bangladesh, AES instituted a benign livestock feed program, without publicity this time, in pursuit of its commitment to environmental responsibility.

As the ten-year anniversary of the Guatemala forestry project approached, AES Thames sent down a dedicated engineer named Dave Burley to see what was going on. Burley was not a world traveler in the usual sense, though he had served nine years in the U.S. Navy on nuclear submarines; he was head of plant maintenance at Thames, a thirteen-year veteran at AES.

Burley was overwhelmed by the poverty of rural Guatemala and disappointed that the trees planted so far were only a fraction of the intended number. But he gradually saw the broader implications and practical effects of the AES-CARE program, the prospects for sustaining good agroforestry practices for farming generations to come. And on the start-up experience of ten years, he reported to his coworkers in Uncasville that the goal of planting trees to absorb the carbon dioxide emissions over the forty-year life span of their power plant could be realized.

"We don't know for sure that it's the right thing to do," Bakke told AES shareholders amid the political controversies over global warming and the responsibilities of the power plants. "But it wasn't the wrong thing to do, no matter what," he argued. In Guatemala, the program put 40,000 farmers to work. "Even if we didn't do a thing for the CO_2 problems of the world, it was more than symbolic. It was something we could do."

Box 5.1

Notes for the Record By Roger Sant (2005)

When AES decided two decades ago that coal would be the fuel of choice for our state-of-the-art power plants, we were obviously not ignorant of the risks—the destructive effects that this plentiful natural fuel had brought upon societies over centuries past. But we also saw clearly the modern technological fixes that could mitigate the damage for generations to come. Our foresight was not 20/20; there were global impacts that we did not foresee.

The basic issue, then as now, is to make the best use of the energy we have available to us, to be efficient in the services to which we put that energy. If some one primary fuel for generating electricity brings along problems not adequately perceived when it was first chosen, then we have to address those problems as we discover them, not negate all the good reasons for choosing that fuel in the first place.

Attractive though non-fossil or renewable fuels are in theory, and I hope in reality soon, the straightforward fact is that without a significant economic subsidy, these alternatives are still nowhere near ready to assume a major role in meeting the nation's demand for electricity. Even with impressive progress in design over the past decade or so, alternative power sources like wind and biomass projects are still serving only limited niches. So much more remains to be done.

The technologies that allowed us to build modern electric power plants—fueled by what we then called "clean coal"—have proved their effectiveness, economic and environmental, against the noxious contaminants that obsolete power plants are spewing into the air across the nation. Those chemical pollutants were at the top of the environmental protection agenda in the 1970s, the targets of the momentous Clear Air Act and its periodic amendments and similar legislative requirements in most of the industrial world. I believe, and do not exaggerate, that as modern power plants come on line to replace the primitive relics of the old electricity industry, these problems of air contamination are virtually disappearing.

I am worried, however, that the policies of the Bush Administration in the early 2000s are delaying that replacement and thus threatening the pace of progress.

Something much broader and more ominous for life on Earth has appeared to trouble us now. Only dimly perceived at the time we started building our plants was the threat of climate change, of global warming, brought about by growing concentrations of greenhouse gasses, primarily CO_2, high in the atmosphere.

Industrial facilities that burn fossil fuels, especially power plants, are major culprits in building up this global threat. AES, I have to say, is one of the largest single emitters of CO_2 in the world. I am proud of the voluntary measures that AES implemented starting in 1987 to offset and mitigate against our own CO_2 emissions, but it was nowhere near enough.

We were never under any illusions that such efforts, undertaken only by those who chose to make them, would be enough. The phenomenon of global warming is too vast to be dealt with by one company or even one country in isolation. Nor is the voluntary gesture, still the refuge chosen by our Administration, viable in the long run.

First is the steep supply curve of carbon mitigation options. Our early efforts, systematic planting of trees and protection of endangered forests, were achieved at an affordable cost of 12 to 15 cents per ton of carbon sequestered. More recent sequestration efforts that others have considered come in many multiples more expensive; fuel substitution and renewables cost well over $5 per ton.

Second, when times were buoyant, it was relatively easy for a company like AES to make voluntary commitments. But when the good times are no longer, with pressures on profitability and liquidity—a company's vital moving parts—even our own AES management finds it is impossible to make further voluntary investments.

Almost everywhere but in the United States, a reasonable scientific and public policy consensus has coalesced about the nature and extent of climate change. We Americans are blocked by interminable delay in implementing potentially corrective measures, such as an international system of carbon taxes or tradable carbon allowances, that would hasten the substitution of conservation and renewable energy for fossil fuels. Fairly imposed, either system would give incentive to individual industries to seek out their own practical steps to compensate for their CO_2 emissions.

Particularly regrettable is the current stance of the United States government, advocating a climate policy based simply on doing more research. Of course there is much we do not yet know about the causes and effects of global warming, but this is no excuse for abandoning government and private-sector leadership in devising least-cost protective measures in the meantime.

I'm attracted to a different, more practical way of confronting global warming, when there is so much we still do not know, yet so daunting is the prospect of what might happen if we do nothing.

This involves a tradable allowance scheme, devised in detail by government and private-sector specialists, in three sequential steps:

1. Agree about the atmospheric greenhouse gas concentration level we would like not to exceed; discussions so far suggest a level, measured in parts per million of CO_2, between 450 and 550.

2. Assign allowances to each country, and subsequently to fuel suppliers within the country, in relation to actual emissions caused by their fuels in, say, 1991; this might give advantage to nations that were in recession at that time, but that is a marginal inequity which just might have to be tolerated.

3. Create a worldwide trading mechanism for buying and selling allowances through existing exchanges, such as the New York Mercantile Exchange.

The European Union is already doing something like this now. They haven't adopted a goal, in terms of global stabilized concentrations, but since they are but a small part of global emissions, it was helpful to get started somewhere.

In 2008, the Kyoto Protocol will expand the EU system to all the signatory nations to that agreement. Is the Kyoto Protocol flawed, as the Bush Administration says? Yes, of course it is, but mainly because it does too little, doesn't include enough nations, and stops in 2018. But it, too, is a start.

In this country, the northeastern states and California, tired of waiting for national leadership, are going ahead with their own plans very similar to those of the EU and Kyoto. Absent the recalcitrance of our federal government, worldwide agreement might well have been achieved by now. Yet with so much in motion, it is only a matter of time—precious time—until that global agreement will have to come.

Of course there will be a cost. But, why can't we look upon it as an insurance policy?

We cannot implement a strategy to stabilize concentrations of greenhouse gasses in the atmosphere for nothing, just as we can't have insurance for nothing. The premium on an insurance policy, however, caps the damages to be suffered if something goes wrong. If all the increasing evidence of global warming continues to reveal the equivalent of a terminal illness in the time ahead, it may become uninsurable. On the other hand, if the dangers of the greenhouse effect turn out to be illusory—an increasingly low probability—no one could fairly complain that we played it safe.

Reasonable people are not faulted for paying reasonable insurance premiums, even if the realities turn out to be less dire than feared. The point is, if we wait until our information is certain and definitive, it will be too late to do anything about it. It's time to get moving.

SIX

The Windshield and the Bug

The first serious tests of AES' corporate values and culture came abruptly in 1992, just as the company was starting to earn standing in the portfolios of adventurous public investors. Two agonizing business crises, themselves unrelated, rudely challenged assumptions that had driven Roger Sant and Dennis Bakke through their first decade of partnership, assumptions about being fair, about having fun on the job, about human nature. They told their new shareholders, "The words of a popular country song seem to fit our view of 1992: 'Sometimes you're the windshield, sometimes you're the bug.'"

After Uncasville in rural Connecticut, AES spotters had identified the Rhode Island town of Woonsocket, then Bucksport on the Penobscot River in Maine, as potential sites for a $350 million cogeneration plant that would replicate the pioneering clean coal technology introduced at AES Thames. In both New England communities, public opposition to a new industrial facility scotched the venture. AES wrote off its $5 million planning and feasibility investment in Bucksport.

AES scouts also found Jacksonville, Florida. There, local authorities and investors seemed interested in a state-of-the-art cogeneration plant to replace the electric output of dirty boilers in an old paper mill that had failed all the environmental tests. AES sent down its ranking expert on circulating fluidized-bed technology, Paul Stinson, control room supervisor at Thames, to try his hand as construction manager of the $485 million Jacksonville power station. Sant and Bakke announced that this facility, to be called AES Cedar Bay, would be "one of the cleanest major solid fuel power plants ever built in Florida, and will contribute significantly to the economic well-being of the city."

The necessary building and environmental permits came through and AES plunged ahead into development, to add a new holding to its portfolio of modern and environmentally responsible power plants.

In May 1992, with construction well under way, an alliance of local residents and state officials challenged the granted permits and accused AES of misleading the public about its intentions for the old paper mill boilers. Unaccustomed to being on the defensive and believing the charges to be false, AES explained its position candidly: "We continue to experience opposition from certain groups in Jacksonville, including many of the city's elected politicians. Some of this is due to our own mistakes; much of it is unavoidable. Regardless, it makes us uncomfortable, since we want to be a positive contributor to the community."

Sant and his AES colleagues still differed, a decade later, about all that went wrong at Cedar Bay. As Sant saw it, the development team, once it had received legal permits, blandly (others say arrogantly) ignored lingering local concerns about the new power plant. Perhaps the lessons of gaining community support from the outset, learned at the early AES plants in California and Connecticut, had not been fully absorbed into the company culture. But possibly the real problem was more prosaic: the paper mill wanted to find a way to use its old boilers, while community activists insisted that the approved plan required unequivocal closing of the out-of-date equipment.

Whatever the mistakes, the consequences were fatal: the State of Florida ordered a halt to construction and initiated a review of the permitting process. Word of the dispute hit the financial news wires, and the value of AES' newly listed stock fell by nearly 20 percent. The banking consortium financing Cedar Bay threatened to pull out, citing an "untenable" political situation. "For nearly three months Sant and other AES people were thoroughly vilified by the opposition and much of the media," wrote Bob Waterman, by this time a company director. "Nobody at AES had fun."

Sant visited Jacksonville for much of every week, belatedly listening to local officials and neighbors and acknowledging AES' role in provoking their anger; Bakke worked the politicians in the state capital, Tallahassee, where his evangelical eloquence for once fell on deaf ears. "We really poured everything we had into defending the honor of the company," Sant said. "We were fighting to protect our values and what we stood for. The veracity of our principles was called into question." The two founders concluded in sorrow that they had failed to "nurture relationships sufficiently with our neighbors at Cedar Bay"—when opposition arose, no community of support was there to speak up on their behalf.

Achieving narrow victories with state authorities, AES nonetheless decided to sell Cedar Bay to another developer, concluding that too much damage had been done to its reputation to make it feasible to continue. The company recovered construction costs but lost the prospect of revenues from yet another innovative power plant.

Some AES people of the period criticized Sant for caving in too quickly to political pressures that could have been fought successfully; his visceral distaste for ugly confrontation had long been recognized as a fact of life in his company. In the case of Cedar Bay, Sant admitted to being worn down by the process, unwilling to let AES appear to be seeking to impose an energy solution on people who said they did not want it.

Six months after AES pulled out, a Florida court dismissed all the claims against Cedar Bay, affirming the integrity of the development plan. The mayor of Jacksonville apologized. Sant and Bakke noted the vindications with relief in their next report to the shareholders but added, "Too bad the court could not give the plant back to us."

The Cedar Bay debacle might have overwhelmed company memory had not a more serious crisis blown up in the same season of that annus horribilis.

The fifth AES power plant, Shady Point, in Poteau, Oklahoma, had started commercial operation in January 1991. At that point it was the largest of the company's coal-burning cogeneration plants, generating 320 megawatts of electricity for a local utility and reusing as much as 100,000 pounds of steam per hour to make dry ice for a nearby chicken processor. Nearly a hundred technicians and engineers, recruited from across the country, relocated to LeFlore County, one of the poorest in Oklahoma, to start new lives with a new employer. On the first year's experience, Sant and Bakke wrote with pride that even workers without previous industrial experience "are making the adjustment to life at AES in a remarkable way." The plant manager, Bill Arnold, a former chemical company executive and manager of AES Deepwater in Houston, was also given the title of corporate vice president.

One of the key components that allowed AES technology to be called "clean coal," operating significantly better than the environmental protection standards, was the process of purifying the water piped through the boilers before returning it to the source, a river or lake nearby. "Our labs regularly test this water to ensure its level of cleanness," declared AES promotional materials.

Not so at Shady Point, as AES headquarters in Arlington suddenly learned in June 1992. A young chemist, a new arrival in eastern Oklahoma, detected discrepancies in the reports of nine employees in the water treatment section; the wastewater discharges may have been contaminated, apparently ever since the plant started operation. Rather than identifying the cause and taking relatively easy steps to correct it, the responsible workers had simply diluted the samples to achieve a satisfactory level for the environmental impact reports.

AES immediately informed the State of Oklahoma and the U.S. Environmental Protection Agency of fraud discovered at Shady Point. "The people involved say they falsified the samples because they feared for their jobs if they reported a violation," the chagrined company leadership explained. The officials called the offense "the sort of minor excursions to be expected during the first year of operation of a new plant"; it could have been easily rectified with timely action—which was not taken.

AES stock, already weakened by the Cedar Bay controversy, was further battered. One-third of the company's market value, some $400 million, evaporated.

The knives were unsheathed against AES on Wall Street, where suspicion of that proclaimed system of corporate values still provoked unease. More peevish analysts found the opportunity to voice long-muffled complaints about the company: a holier-than-thou attitude, arrogance, and naïveté regarding employees and investors. "They talked about corporate values and their responsibilities toward employees, but what about their responsibilities toward shareholders?" complained one investment advisor.

"When we publicly commit to strive for excellence . . . and then fall short," Sant and Bakke replied, "criticism seems stronger and more biting than if we had been quieter or had lower standards—no one complains when things are going great." On a Sunday in the midst of the crisis, Sant and Bob Hemphill drafted a letter to the nearly 400 employees of AES:

> We thought we had explained our values enough to everyone in AES that this sort of thing could never happen here. We are trying to treat people like adults, trusting in their honesty, judgment, maturity and professionalism— rather than relying on detailed procedures, manuals, and minute supervisory oversight. We cannot comprehend why anyone would trade our integrity to make our environmental performance look better. . . . [We are] embarrassed and disappointed and angry that this could have happened in AES.

Later Sant reflected, "If it had been one person falsifying reports, we could have made the case that he or she was a bad seed. But with nine people, we had to accept that the problem was systemic."

The guilty workers were not fired. (Long afterward, Sant wondered if this show of compassion was a mistake, a failure to insist on personal accountability no matter how much respect is accorded to the individual.) They were demoted to lower-paying jobs that included sensitivity training in the law and in company values and culture. Making good on their promise of integrity as defined in the company's values statement—"All that we do and say in all parts of the company fit together with truth and consistency"— the entire leadership at AES headquarters accepted cuts in their annual pay, ranging from 3 percent for those not directly involved with Shady Point to 24 percent or more for the top executives, Sant and Bakke included. All company employees took the hit, with reductions in their profit-sharing and stock option allotments for the year.

Subsequent government investigations revealed that, despite the admitted falsification of the reports, the wastewater returned to the Poteau River had not been contaminated after all. AES readily paid the minimum fine of $125,000 for falsifying EPA reports. By the end of the year, the company's stock price had recovered to its level before the Shady Point fraud.

Painful as the financial impact was, what stung Roger Sant, Dennis Bakke, and their loyalists the most was the blatant affront to an operating culture they had sought to instill throughout their company. The fundamental shock to AES assumptions about management, trust, and human capacity could not be easily healed.

Bakke took most of the hits. He was, after all, chief operating officer, but he had also emerged as evangelist for the company's cultural values, even more so than Sant. Bakke minced no words about the bitter residue that he endured for two years following the Shady Point incident. Outside board members, pounded by the suspicions of Wall Street financiers and lawyers, warned bluntly that Bakke's time at AES had come and gone, that his continuing tenure was damaging the company. Sant listened patiently to the complaints, but felt the situation was salvageable. As Bakke told it, "The board and others started saying, 'OK, your experiment is over. It failed. It's time to revert to the traditional way of doing things.'" The "traditional way," of course, meant a more hierarchical organization, with lines of authority and supervision clearly delineated and enforced. To Sant and Bakke, this would only debase the culture of "ownership," of individual responsibility and dignity, that they had long proclaimed.

The founders had heard the argument many times from investment advisors and bankers on Wall Street. But this time they also heard it from within AES—from the workers in Oklahoma, who began venting their discomfort with and suspicions about the high-sounding principles Bakke preached so fervently whenever he visited the plant. They resented derogatory comparisons between the AES people at Thames in Connecticut (implication: those who "got it") and the people at Shady Point in Oklahoma (implication: those who didn't).

The Shady Point crews demanded straightforward shift supervisors as in any other industrial facility, along with specialized functional departments for planning, environmental regulation, and safety. To prevent any more rogue violations, for which they would all have to pay, they called for a reorganization of the plant into the traditional ladders of responsibility and centralized authority: no more of this "honeycomb" stuff.

The plant manager, Bill Arnold, defending the AES cultural values, tried to channel the workers' discomfort back onto the AES track, but his dilemma was just as stark as Bakke's. If AES truly believed in respecting and empowering its employees to solve their own operational problems, how could the home office resist pressure from a local crew to take steps that executives did not like?

"Striking a balance between being sensitive to legitimate, helpful critiques . . . while sticking to the fundamental approaches that have made this such a fun and successful place to work has been difficult," Sant and Bakke wrote in a joint letter early in 1993. "This is no doubt a healthy struggle, but one that added considerable stress and some pain to our efforts these recent months."

Bakke felt more than "some" pain, and probably doubted the healthiness of it all, when one day in the midst of the struggle he received a telephone call from plant manager Arnold, conveying in sadness the outcome of an all-plant meeting: the request that Dennis Bakke pay no further visits to Shady Point.

"They 'fired' me," the bruised chief operating officer said—in an interview— itself a rather remarkable development within a modern corporation. He spent much of the next four months in heart-to-heart sessions with AES people at offices and power plants across the company (but not, to his sadness, at Shady Point), seeking advice on how all the competing interests could be balanced.

Sant, ever the problem solver, tried to mediate the confrontation and resisted all calls for Bakke's resignation. Impassioned discussions proceeded at all levels of the company on matters of social, psychological, regional, and cultural concerns within a growing and far-flung organization. Bakke, at Sant's urging, met individually with each member of the board and pledged to be more open to their concerns about the company's management. From outside, intrigued business school faculties tuned in to a crisis of corporate governance in a uniquely high-minded company.

Over the months, the Shady Point crews reached their own basic, and unexpected, conclusion: the "conventional and safe" hierarchical organization they had demanded might well serve to protect them from criticism whenever something went wrong, but no so-called good management practices could protect them from people, themselves or their coworkers, when they made mistakes.

"The AES people at the plant have taken some reasonable risks to keep ultimate responsibility for adherence to the shared values of integrity, fairness and social responsibility with individuals and the 'family groups,'" Sant and Bakke wrote in their 1993 annual report—they avoided the loaded "honeycomb" word. "The resulting ownership, freedom and accountability at the team level gives them the best chance to maximize another shared value— fun—as well."

Through all the turmoil, the Shady Point plant continued doing its job at an extraordinary level of operational efficiency, generating electricity for lights, appliances, and air conditioners through the hot Oklahoma summer. Its level of availability came in at 99.7 percent, in all likelihood an all-time performance record for a large coal-fired power plant.

A year or so after his stern message to Bakke, Bill Arnold again called Arlington from Oklahoma, this time to say, after the latest all-plant meeting, "Dennis, we hereby invite you to visit Shady Point. We have decided to come back to AES."

The bitter shock to AES' founding culture from the experiences of 1992 brought a broader mood of inquiry throughout the company, from the executive offices to the plant floors. Internal management issues—honeycomb or hierarchy, decentralized or top-down responsibility, fairness and fun— were obvious flash points, but executives and hard-hat workers alike became curious about the most basic of AES values. What, exactly, does "social responsibility" mean to a company working in a competitive, free-market world?

In 1993, back from a trip to Pakistan, Sant told an audience at Harvard University that his sense of the company's values had undergone refinement. Planting trees to reduce the concentration of carbon dioxide in the atmosphere, the AES initiative for which Harvard was honoring him, "misses the goal of social responsibility to the people around us," he said. Definition of "the environment" took broader meaning; it had to include the local community that a company was joining. Schools, health care, and housing may well surpass global warming in the concerns of the people in the community. If AES wants to be socially responsible, can it overlook things that people want and need?

Roger Naill wrote a down-to-earth memo in May 1994 to provoke internal discussion at AES. "Up until now, [social responsibility] has pretty much been defined as, Do CO_2 offsets plus anything else you need to do locally to get the project done." Maybe the time had come to broaden a pragmatic business instinct into a thoughtful set of corporate values.

Naill had been one of Sant's original hires, for his skills in computer modeling; he had gradually moved into the role of in-house deep thinker, finding kinship with Bakke in their shared zeal to do good in the world (he had not even met Bakke before joining AES). Lest anyone think that he was just sounding off again, he explained that "Dennis asked me to help us think through, as a group, what this new commitment means in practical terms."

> The AES value of "social responsibility" as applied to a project means that we are committed to go beyond legal and political requirements to mitigate social problems: we want to do more than the minimum. We want AES projects to be socially beneficial, not harmful or even neutral. If an AES project causes any significant social harm, we have an obligation to mitigate that harm. . . . When people think of the power project, what should come to mind is "this AES project provides real social benefits," not negative impacts.

With that as his starting point, and recognizing all the other values in the AES culture, Naill suggested that the leadership of each power plant or project decide how to live up to community obligations—not rigidly adhering to priorities defined by executives in Arlington.

> As a part of the process of getting "educated" on this issue, the plant/project team might ask experts in this field and interested parties inside and outside the company, . . . partners, local and national policymakers, local and national experts, and local citizens (including groups that might easily be excluded—e.g., women or minorities).

The process would force hard judgments: give priority to mitigating global warming or to ensuring clean water for the neighborhood? Improve local schools and provide affordable housing, offering employment opportunities and tangible economic impact on the community? "Should we keep 'social responsibility' narrowly focused on things that mitigate societal problems *caused by the plant*, or focus more broadly"—on social problems that would exist whether or not the AES plant were there?

The best guide for these decisions, Naill concluded, is the *consciences* of the men and women working at the plant, many of whom had relocated to live in the community. Let our conscience be our guide: "Have we done enough? Are there any remaining detrimental impacts of our plant that we should mitigate?"

The Naill inquiry posed hard questions for AES people at every level, encouraged as they were to take personal responsibility for the "wholeness" of the company, for everything their company did.

Ken Woodcock, the pragmatic developer working down the hall from Naill and one of the original Sant-Bakke faithful, accepted the issue of social responsibility as a "potential deal-breaker." In considering any new project, AES had to figure in what he called the "fatal flaw" analysis, Woodcock argued. Any new proposal "should recommend what extra actions should be taken to make the project have net social benefits." An audit of social responsibility (however defined) should be undertaken by the project team *before* the commitment to go ahead, not as an afterthought. "We should have some confidence that the project can be done in a socially responsible way *before* we spend lots of money."

This kind of soul-searching in executive suites, in power plant control rooms, and among the crews who ran the turbines was not generally known to the investing public, nor was it of much interest to the financial managers who recommended—or shunned—commitment to that strange company called AES. The typical businessperson would very likely have been incredulous to discover that a public profit-making corporation was spending any of its time and talent on issues seemingly irrelevant to the bottom line.

At the same time, self-examination of a more traditional sort was under way in the congenial corridors of Arlington and on the floors of the power plants. Sant called it a "recontexting," and its outcome was the opening of a spectacular new business era for AES.

SEVEN

A New Context

As a business school professor, Roger Sant had always pressed upon the aspiring entrepreneurs in his classes a notion he called "recontexting"—the process of challenging all working assumptions, even in boom times; reexamining the foundations for decisions; and exploring ways to try new things or even new ways to do old, familiar things. At the time, managing his own company and ever considering it a work in progress, he would tell his colleagues, "I worry if too much time has passed when we haven't had a big context shift."

The 1990s brought a bewildering series of context changes as small companies suddenly found themselves operating within a global framework. The previous decade had been auspicious for radical innovations in the electric power industry, building upon the "disruptive" new opportunities opened by the Public Utility Regulatory Policies Act of 1978 (PURPA). AES had made the most of them. In one decade, Roger Sant and Dennis Bakke's upstart enterprise had grown from an idea, in a new atmosphere of deregulation, to the operator of four state-of-the-art power plants plus one complete refurbishment (the old synthetic rubber plant at Beaver Valley, Pennsylvania), with two more under construction. These physical assets, valued at $1.4 billion, were capable of generating more than a thousand megawatts of electricity to power homes, offices, and stores from Hawaii to Connecticut, from California and Pennsylvania to Texas and Oklahoma.

Plate No.1. Roger Sant and Dennis Bakke at an AES project review in Arlington, Virginia, October 1982.

Plate No.2. Vicki Sant at an AES project review in Arlington, Virginia, October 1982.

Plate No.3. Roger Sant at the construction site of AES' first generating plant, AES Deepwater, a 140-megawatt petroleum coke–fired facility in Houston, Texas, 1984.

Plate No.4. Roger Sant (left) and Dennis Bakke (right) with Bob Hemphill on Roger's dock at Donner Lake, California, 1987. Key decisions relative to AES values and culture were made at this meeting.

Plate No.5. Roger Sant speaking at the groundbreaking ceremony for AES Shady Point, a 320-megawatt coal-fired circulating fluidized-bed facility in Poteau, Oklahoma, September 3, 1987. Seated at right is Patrick J. Ryan, executive vice president of Oklahoma Gas and Electric Company.

Plate No.6. Michelle Brawner and Tom
Tribone at a company gathering, January 1988.

Plate No.7. The New England development team: Stu Ryan (seated) with
(from left) Michelle Brawner, Brently Davis, Ann Murtlow, and Lenny Lee,
1989.

Plate No.8. The board of directors at the 1992 dedication of AES Barbers Point, a 180-megawatt coal-fired plant in Hawaii. From left, Bob Waterman, Russ Train, Dennis Bakke, Roger Sant, Henry Linden, Art Rolander, Tom Unterberg, and Frank Jungers.

Plate No.9. Dennis Bakke and Roger Sant, November 1993, on the night Roger announced that Dennis would become chief executive officer of AES.

Plate No.10. Plant manager Dave McMillen and Roger Sant at AES Thames, Connecticut, 1993.

Plate No.11. Paul Tatum and Roger Sant during a plant visit at AES Deepwater, 1994.

Plate No.12. Roger Sant and Shahzad Qasim, group manager for the Middle East, November 16, 1994, at the opening of a government-operated middle school for girls donated by AES Lal Pir, a 360-megawatt oil-fired generating facility in Pakistan.

Plate No.13. Dennis Bakke and Roger Sant at an AES board meeting in Hawaii, 1994.

Plate No.14. Roger Sant (right) and Kerry Yeager (left) at the home of Shimon Peres, Israel's minister of foreign affairs, 1994.

Plate No.15. Dave McMillen (left) with his wife, Beverly, and Roger Sant in 1996. McMillen was responsible for adapting the AES values to plant operations, first at AES Thames, a 180-megawatt coal-fired cogeneration facility in Montville, Connecticut, and later at AES Shady Point in Oklahoma.

Plate No.16. At the listing of AES on the New York Stock Exchange, October 16, 1996. From left, Barry Sharp, executive vice president and chief financial officer; Roger Naill, vice president; Dennis Bakke; Ken Woodcock, executive vice president; John Ruggirello, executive vice president; Alice (Tish) Emerson, board member; Roger Sant; and Bill Johnston, president of the NYSE.

Plate No.17. Roger Sant (right) and Mark Fitzpatrick at an AES orientation in Budapest, Hungary, 1999.

Plate No.18. Roger Sant and Pakistan's president, Pervez Musharraf, Lahore, 2000.

Plate No. 19. From left, president and chief executive officer Paul Hanrahan with his wife, Rodanthe, and former executive vice president Mark Fitzpatrick with his wife, Patty, 2001.

Assets in the power industry are an important traditional measure of potential earnings. Sant and Bakke reminded their investors that "asset-intensive companies are generally perceived to be quite risky." To the contrary, they argued a different analysis:

> We believe there are reasons that such a generalization does not apply to AES. Even though our assets to sales ratio is high, the risk of that position is offset by long term contracts insuring revenues for each project, the non-recourse nature of each of our project financings, and the steps we take to hedge our costs relative to our revenues. Indeed, we are probably much less risky than non-capital intensive companies our size—a paradox if one is used to thinking conventionally.

AES' 1991 profits reached $42.6 million, an increase of 155 percent over the year before. Unlike a typical growth company, AES opted to pay dividends to shareholders rather than accumulate cash reserves for future business development. The unconventional Sant-Bakke business plan had presumed to achieve success in management and operations without substantial cash input—a good thing, too, if it could be made to work, for at start-up their company had no cash. Then, as earnings mounted, the cofounders turned necessity into strategy:

> If we were to accumulate cash, we are concerned that the availability of our own funds might actually reduce our discipline to structure projects creatively for non-recourse financing or avoid projects that cannot stand financial market scrutiny.

Sant's declared goal was to pay out each year's earnings in dividends within one year of the money's being earned, though he acknowledged that irregularity in cash flow and reserve requirements under project loan agreements might not make this workable as a firm commitment.

In the nonfinancial context, and despite the perennial environmental concerns, coal remained the company's fuel of choice. AES executives assembled masses of empirical data to persuade skeptics that their modern plants burned the legendary dirty fuel far more cleanly than ever before: emissions of noxious nitrogen oxides and sulfur dioxide (SO_2) across the AES plants averaged 70 percent and 48 percent, respectively—*below* the levels permitted under the federal Clean Air Act.

There remained, of course, carbon dioxide (CO_2) and related greenhouse gases emitted by power plants that were not addressed by the Clean Air Act. AES was experimenting with innovative ways to deal with them, too (see chapter 5), though many years will pass before results can be measured definitively.

In sum, during the 1980s AES became the largest of the new deregulated power producers in the United States, as measured in generating capacity. More than three dozen competitors had sprung up to seize the opportunity offered by the PURPA legislation. Together they created a new industry sector independent of the regulated utilities, which had long been the only serious players in the electricity business. And these utility monopolies were managing to overcome their initial suspicions of the competitive newcomers, beginning to see self-interest in a competitive wholesale market for electricity. They would reap the benefits of not having to build their own generating capacity for short-term or even long-term increases in demand.

The new deregulated sector had incentives to build sophisticated power plants to replace the crumbling electricity factories of the past, as the protected monopolies did not. AES alone offered about 15 percent of all the new cogeneration power capacity; by the end of the 1980s, the independent power sector as a whole provided more than 35 percent of new capacity, and the portion grew to half within the next couple of years according to the calculations of *Electricity Journal.* With competition came efficiencies and economies. Sant could show that the price of electricity to customers of the new high-technology power plants had dropped by nearly half in the decade after 1983.

At the start of the 1990s, AES had become a new winner in an old game. But the size and shape of the playing field demanded prudence. The electricity industry was enormous and entrenched. The newcomers began from a standing start. This made the growth statistics look impressive, but growth was distributed among dozens of competing players.

Reality check: AES may have been the biggest independent power producer, but this one company's total capacity was only 6.6 percent of the
deregulated sector's output, according to the calculations of *Electricity Journal*,
and the new sector as a whole provided only 3.3 percent of the electricity
demanded by the American economy. The long head start of the utility
monopolies and their massive old infrastructure was obviously not to be overcome in a single decade.

At their company's ten-year mark, Sant and Bakke advised fellow investors
of "interesting changes" in the environment of power generation. Nothing of
either great value or great danger had shown up to alter a business plan in
progress, they said, but interesting changes were indeed in the making.

First of all, cogeneration, the technology enshrined in the PURPA statute
to put the waste product of steam to a second productive use, was turning out
to be financially irrelevant. Revenues from the otherwise wasted steam were
trivial compared with those from the electricity generated. The siting of new
power plants still depended on a nearby steam customer to meet the requirements for federal deregulation, but contracts for the sale of steam were no
longer a significant factor in economic viability.

Second was the growing competition in the business AES had pioneered, those
dozens of new independent power producers springing up across the country on
the AES pattern or something resembling it. Already by 1989 the electric capacity
they offered the utilities exceeded by ten times the capacity requested. Those early
optimistic projections of supply and demand had been a bit off; the demand for electricity had dropped far below the exponential growth rate forecast in the models.

The cost of electricity to consumers was dropping—a welcome tribute
to the efficacy of competition, but something less than a bonanza for the
income statements of the generating companies. Perhaps the virtues of energy
conservation argued by Sant, Sawhill, and their colleagues back in the 1970s
were taking hold too well for the growth curves of the power generators.

After hesitating over the political and environmental concerns, AES' competitors eventually reached the same calculations in choosing coal as their
fuel of choice: the number of new cogeneration power plants burning coal

doubled during the 1980s, from 12 percent to 25 percent of newly built plants. But with lingering community uneasiness about coal dust in the air, by 1992 Sant and Bakke reluctantly concluded that "coal projects are very difficult to site anywhere in the U.S."

The measure and engine for operating growth in the independent power sector is the number of new electricity contracts that a company can sign per year. The brutal fact, as Sant's ten-year recontexting effort got under way, was that AES had signed not a single new electricity contract in 1990—and this was the second consecutive year of the slowdown.

These unwelcome facts made their impact on the capital markets. Over its first decade, AES could operate on what the enthusiasts called the "field of dreams" strategy: "If you build the businesses, the financing will come." Ever candid, even in prosaic financial reports, Sant and Bakke declared in their 1991 annual report, "Every financing of a new plant seems to us a unique miracle." In the new context, the commercial banks and equity investors, which had been so forthcoming in the early years of an exciting new business concept, were growing skittish. The obvious alternative sources of capital financing—insurance companies and pension funds, which, like the power plants, are structured on a long time horizon—were reluctant to step into untested, still somewhat exotic, enterprises. (An exception was AES Cedar Bay, where a large insurer had joined the financing package. The troubles of that business did nothing to encourage further commitments from insurance companies.)

National energy policy was also undergoing interesting changes. Ten years or so after Roger Sant first outlined the novel idea, the least-cost energy strategy was gaining widespread support. "By 1990," wrote Paul L. Joskow of the Massachusetts Institute of Technology, "least cost planning was all the rage among state regulatory commissions and was spreading quickly from its origins in California, the Northeast and the Northwest."

The 1978 legislation that started the restructuring of the American electricity industry was being overtaken by technology and public sentiment. The new independent power producers and the old regulated utilities were at one in calling for the repeal of PURPA, or at least fundamental updating, from the lessons learned in a decade of practical experience.

The utilities still chafed under the statutory requirement to pay high "avoided costs" for power offered by the unregulated new companies, which were thus generating big profits as well as cheaper electricity. For their part, these "disruptive" entrants into the marketplace sought relief from the requirement to pursue the technology of cogeneration, a good idea that was proving largely meaningless in terms of both economics and environmental protection. (PURPA can thus be considered a signal of the futility of enshrining in law a specific technique in a rapidly changing industry, harbinger of the computer software litigations a decade later.)

The Energy Policy Act of 1992 refined the PURPA reforms as suggested by experience but offered no retreat from the principles of a competitive free market in electricity. Indeed, specific new openings for competition were defined, notably in provisions for "wholesale transmission access." This secured the place of the independents in the business of generating power, but it also opened the way for a new business pursuit, perhaps even more disruptive than the earlier functional separation of generating power from transmitting and distributing power. This was the business of "power trading."

AES was not the only company, though it was probably the first, to be granted statutory license to trade power, just like any other commodity. The seller of electricity, in this scheme of things, did not itself have to generate the power, as AES had set out to do; it could act as a broker, buying contracts for supply of electricity and selling contracts for the sales.

Signing up a few experienced commodity traders, Sant and Bakke's company set up a computerized trading floor in Atlanta for a venture into domestic power brokering, called AES Power. They informed their shareholders in the 1993 annual report:

A team of our people is attempting to link companies that have power to sell with those that need power. This venture can be successful only if our people learn immense amounts about the market for electricity— when it's needed, where the extra capacity is, what the transmission possibilities are—and establish trusting relationships with both buyers and sellers. It is far too early to forecast our success but we are learning a great deal about the market.

What they learned was not entirely to their liking. First, a complex marketplace does not emerge at any level of efficiency and integrity overnight; rather, it takes years to mature. Power trading, like any commodity-trading business, requires rapid actions and decisions by relatively junior employees staring at computer terminals and tracing constantly changing price patterns. Millions of dollars could be made or lost in a few seconds. Yet not for four full years after the 1992 enabling act were the rules for the marketplace introduced, and it took three more years to make them final. Neither Sant nor Bakke could see much of a place for AES in this anarchy.

Second, any fast-moving brokerage operation demands a layer of supervision, maybe several layers, by senior officers exercising almost minute-by-minute scrutiny over high-pressure operations in which opportunities and temptations for quick profits (and losses) abound. This kind of supervisory oversight went entirely against the AES culture, with its emphasis on the autonomy and responsibility of the individual worker.

In short, after scarcely a year in trial operation, AES closed down its brokerage subsidiary, making the strategic decision to abandon the power-trading business in favor of the more familiar business of building and managing power plants.

Competitors in the independent power sector, notably the Enron Corporation of Houston, reached the opposite conclusion: it sold off tangible assets in the form of power plants (AES bought a few of them) in order to focus its cash and human resources on a highly leveraged power-trading brokerage, in which bigger and quicker profits could be made.

When the bubble burst in 2001 and Enron was forced into bankruptcy and a wave of criminal indictments, AES' decision to back away from the power-trading market could have been cited as a brilliant flash of business acumen and integrity. But as the independent power sector enjoyed its spectacular growth spurt in the 1990s, AES made enough of its own bad calls, destructive business mistakes that allowed no room for satisfaction about its decision to abandon the little experiment called AES Power.

Recontexting had its personal side. Over the decade, Roger Sant had become a person of unique stature: a successful executive of the power industry who was at the same time a dedicated environmentalist. It was, after all, their passion for environmental protection that first lured Sant and his wife, Vicki, to Washington, DC, and the career path that culminated in the AES Corporation.

Sant found himself in constant demand as a speaker at academic and professional conferences and as a provider of pro bono service on boards of environmental groups, where he was eager to offer practical business and financial expertise. Even as chief executive officer of AES, he served as volunteer chairman of the Environmental and Energy Study Institute and vice chairman of the World Resources Institute, the private think tank that stimulated his concern over global warming and helped AES design its innovative program to plant trees to mitigate the emissions of its power plants. Roger and Vicki established their own private philanthropy, the Summit Foundation, to support the causes in which they fervently believed.

At the same time, two major environmental organizations were courting this sympathetic power industry executive for their own leadership, and, to Sant's discomfort, both were directed by individuals whom he considered mentors.

After leaving government service and tiring of McKinsey energy consulting projects, John Sawhill had gone to the venerable Nature Conservancy, an organization engaged in buying and protecting delicate land in the United States for conservation purposes. Then there was the World Wildlife Fund, headed by a towering figure in environmentalism, Russell Train. Train, a former head of the U.S. Environmental Protection Agency, had supported Sant's research at Carnegie Mellon University and had become a founding director of AES. WWF managed a network of some three hundred field-workers directing programs to support biodiversity and ecosystems around the world.

Sant had to choose between the two institutions; he could not offer both the time and energy they would require while also serving as CEO of an expanding corporation. He used to quip that he had never before held a full-time job for longer than three years, yet after a full decade at AES he remained totally committed to the company and insisted that he was still having fun on the job.

Hardly obscure in the wings, however, was his chosen successor at AES. From the start of their joint venture, Dennis Bakke had been in effect the chief operating officer of the innovative enterprise they had founded together. "It was always obvious to me," Sant said, "that Dennis would grow into the leadership of our company, though we didn't talk about it much and the only question was when it would happen."

Unlike Sant, Bakke did not automatically command confidence among AES' board of directors and major shareholders. Only after four years was the company's young, dynamic cofounder elected to membership on the board, and two more years would pass before he was promoted from executive vice president to president of AES (with Sant remaining as chairman and CEO).

Bakke, the self-styled inside man during the company's growing years, was rewarded with intense devotion and loyalty from the headquarters staff. He was brisk and decisive in his business judgments, though he would proudly proclaim that his style of management was to make no more than one operating decision a year, leaving the rest to the men and women in the field. But to some of the company's directors and major investors, Bakke's flair for the dramatic, his zeal in preaching values and social responsibility, often came across as self-righteous grandstanding. Recall how employees of the Shady Point power plant "fired" him, as Bakke himself put it, from their plant.

Facing the challenges of that annus horribilis, Sant temporarily pulled away from his time commitments to environmental activism. He delayed the transfer of executive authority at AES until his protégé could gain the confidence of the skeptics. But by the end of 1993, he had decided that the time and context had come to begin a gradual transition. He stepped down as CEO in Bakke's favor, though he remained the company's chairman and a full-time member, along with Bob Hemphill and Bakke himself, of the "office of the CEO."

The founding partnership continued without interruption for four more years. Sant became the working chairman of the World Wildlife Fund, but most days he was in Arlington or traveling for AES—sharing responsibility for AES operations. The adjoining office doors at the AES headquarters were still left open.

Sant's informal recontexting episode reached its climax at the start of the 1990s—none too soon for a newly visible public company properly concerned about the quality of revenues and cash flow under the founders' original business plan. Context is a wide and broadening horizon. The 1990s brought a new situation that the visionary founders of AES had not anticipated.

AES had been born of intellectual ferment brought about by the rethinking and restructuring of the power industry triggered by the energy crisis of the 1970s, and a growing concern for social responsibility in corporate governance. A third source of ferment was becoming a global trend as the 1990s came into view; it defined AES' direction and operations into the twenty-first century.

For forty years after the end of World War II, not only countries under communist control but also the Western social democracies had developed on the theory that governments could properly and effectively manage their national economies. By the 1980s, a new era was emerging worldwide in which competition, deregulation, and privatization of state assets, as economic historian Daniel Yergin wrote, had captured world economic thinking.

In the new theory, national infrastructure assets, previously considered a proper holding of government, became "products" to be put up for sale to private enterprises and operated by them in a competitive free market. State-owned electric power systems became prime candidates for such privatization because at first they seemed less vulnerable to populist concerns than more visible consumer industries. "Many of these systems are highly inefficient and would operate more productively and provide more reliable service under private ownership," argued Jerry L. Pfeffer, an academic advisor to the electricity industry.

Ahead of the curve, AES had started exploring business opportunities abroad as early as 1987, just as its first power plants in the United States were coming online. Sant and Bakke called this the start of their own learning curve. The company opened its first foreign office in 1988 in London, where

Prime Minister Margaret Thatcher was preaching the ideology of privatization and competition.

As in the United States earlier, the British government was studying the complex process of separating the generation of electricity from its transmission and distribution. AES had credibility in explaining how this process (albeit under different evolutionary circumstances) was proceeding across the Atlantic. And the nimble newcomers signaled their interest in transplanting the AES management culture abroad, in existing power plants as well as new state-of-the-art facilities. Sant made almost monthly trips to the United Kingdom to work his skills of persuasion on as many of Britain's twelve state-owned distribution utilities as would give him a hearing.

Thatcher's government privatized the Central Electricity Generating Board (also state owned) in 1989, and the lines were drawn for a test of whether the American experience could be made viable in other nations and economies. In May 1992, in a joint venture with the entrepreneurial Belgian utility Tractebel, AES spent $415 million to acquire its first overseas business: two old oil- and coal-burning power plants in Northern Ireland called Belfast West and Kilroot, with a combined output of 640 megawatts. From this British base, AES scouts began seeking opportunities in the industrialized world from Norway to New Zealand, where the same drive toward a competitive free market in electricity was gaining momentum. AES was one of four power companies chosen to bid for development of a new 600-megawatt coal-burning facility in Perth, Australia; had it won, this would have been the largest greenfield power plant AES had yet built.

At the same time, unexpected opportunities began appearing in lands long closed to American entrepreneurship in infrastructure, the old Soviet satellites of eastern Europe. With the cold war regimes crumbling (the Berlin Wall fell in 1989), the postcommunist leaders looked to the West for help in cleaning up their decrepit and dirty electricity systems, among the many monuments to communist economic failure.

Sant's recontexting at the turn of the 1990s faced a decreased demand for electricity in the United States, and with it a decreased demand for new power plants, however efficient and environmentally sound they might be.

At the same time, in much of the world overseas, the demand for electricity was growing. "Many foreign markets have 'leap-frogged' the U.S.," Sant argued in the scholarly *Electricity Journal*, "putting in place competitive market structures that are more aggressive than the one existing in the U.S."

One overseas office in London would no longer suffice. Arlington headquarters established a new business division under Hemphill's direction, AES Transpower, to seek out business opportunities in developing countries, where demand for electricity was growing two to three times faster than in the industrialized countries. AES Transpower's operating manager was a newcomer to the company's executive ranks, Paul Hanrahan, a graduate of the naval academy at Annapolis and of Harvard Business School who had served five years on nuclear submarines.

Hemphill and Hanrahan developed an innovative plan to build a string of small power plants in China, in the six major coal-producing provinces upstream from Shanghai and down toward Guangzhou. Late in 1992, AES reached a preliminary understanding with a state utility in India, "a burgeoning market," Sant and Bakke told their shareholders, "if we can figure out how to serve it."

An industry sector that had emerged from an act of the United States Congress was now presuming to make its way in a wider world. Acquisition and transformation of old power plants in far-flung lands had hardly been in Sant and Bakke's original business plan, but on every continent they saw electricity infrastructure badly in need of modernization. This was something that AES had shown it could do.

"How can we *not* be there?" Sant said, amid all the frustrations and setbacks of attempting to do business in unfamiliar settings. "If we're in the power business, we have to go where the demand is."

EIGHT

Power to the World

Prime Minister Margaret Thatcher's economic team in London may have been setting the pace for overhaul in the industrialized social democracies. But half a world away, another brain trust was forming, with local business support, to figure out how a competitive free market could take hold in the public and private sectors of lagging developing nations as well. The demand for basic services, including electricity, was enormous; the state-owned infrastructure for meeting the demand was, at best, feeble.

The new thinking began in Córdoba, Argentina. Led by a son of the town named Domingo Cavallo, an irreverent Harvard-trained economist, the Córdoba research institute IEERAL (Instituto de Estudios Económicos sobre la Realidad Argentina y Latinoamericana) defined a reform agenda for national economic renewal. Its key planks were elimination of protectionist trade barriers; pegging of the Argentine currency to the dollar, to encourage foreign investment and prevent any populist political leadership from manipulating the exchange rate; and, as in Thatcher's formula, the sale of bloated state-owned enterprises to private managers, who, better than government bureaucracies, could introduce efficiency, productivity, and customer satisfaction. Nowhere did these virtues seem more needed than in the supply of electricity to home and commerce.

Cavallo became one of Latin America's most influential economists for a time, and IEERAL's agenda was embraced in what was called the "Washington consensus." The term was a misnomer; unlike strategies of previous decades to realize the hemispheric growth potential, the primary impetus came from Latin American nations themselves, not the overpowering giant up north. The unfortunate label seemed to confer a stature of legitimacy for American government and private-sector interests at the turn of the 1990s as they were seeking to tap the natural and human resources of the long-faltering nations to the south.

AES was but one of the aggressive independent power-producing companies turning their sights on Argentina, as a test case, and then beyond. Tom Tribone, a senior vice president after his entrepreneurship at Beaver Valley in Pennsylvania, Placerita in California, and other early AES ventures, became the company's point man for Latin America. He arranged to meet Cavallo for thoughtful discussion and, not surprisingly, seized upon the impulse for privatization of state-owned electric industries. Argentina, he discovered, was ahead of even Thatcher's Britain in willingness to open not only electricity generation but also transmission and distribution to foreign investment. AES' competitors, such as Southern Electric International and Duke Energy, were moving to acquire hydroelectric generating plants and even an interest in the country's transmission grid.

In May 1993, AES completed the purchase of a one-third share in the 650-megawatt plant Central Térmica San Nicolás, just south of Buenos Aires, and proposed to its partners a complete staff reorganization along AES principles of autonomy and workers' responsibility.

Modest and troublesome San Nicolás signaled a major commitment by AES to the Latin American ("Washington") consensus for free-market economic renewal, a commitment that grew to embrace Brazil, Venezuela, Chile, Peru, Bolivia, and Colombia. Over the coming years, as the Argentine economy failed to respond to imperfectly implemented Cavallo reforms and nearby countries struggled with the Argentine downdraft, AES began aggressively buying privatized assets, including even the interests of those early

American competitors who were growing disillusioned at the lack of progress. In Brazil alone, AES eventually invested more than $4 billion, becoming the largest private investor in the Brazilian electricity industry. Brazil contributed more than a quarter of AES' worldwide revenues, more than all AES receivables from plants and businesses in the United States.

Latin America was a strategic commitment that cost AES dearly when the bubble of earnings growth burst in 2001.

Just as the 1980s had seen the emergence of an independent power-generating sector in the United States, the 1990s saw the birth of what could be called International Electricity, a multinational, multi-billion-dollar industry reporting double-digit growth rates. In financial and political clout around the world, it remained puny compared with fabled International Oil, nearly a century in the building. But, as Roger Sant always took pains to explain, such dubious power status was never in the sector's sights or capabilities. The entrepreneurs of electricity were simply responding to opportunities and needs as they appeared.

In the United States back in the early 1980s, independent power projects could be devised to yield internal rates of return of 30 to 50 percent, reported the *Electricity Journal* a decade later. "These 'gold rush' days are over." By the 1990s, overseas ventures, particularly in emerging market economies, appeared as attractive alternatives, offering expected returns far higher than were then available in the United States.

A prominent AES competitor, Charles Goff, head of Destec Energy, put it bluntly to a conference of utility executives: American independent power producers were moving beyond the United States market "because there is less risk in other countries—something I thought I would never hear."

From May 1992 to the end of 1993, AES had grown from a domestic company with a fledgling link to the United Kingdom (Northern Ireland) to an international company with "activity" (to be sure, not yet productive businesses) in no fewer than seventeen countries.

Sant grew reflective as he prepared to turn over the responsibilities of company leadership to Dennis Bakke at the end of 1993. Writing in professional journals and in his final annual report as CEO, he reviewed the course of the AES "learning curve" that had started in Britain six years before. His points may have seemed modest and restrained when he first made them, but they were revisited with analytic rhetoric in scholarly studies for years to follow.

In the first place, asserting the AES emphasis on having fun on the job, Sant quoted one of his executives who had been on the road seeking new business opportunities:

It's sure a lot more fun negotiating with someone in Nanchang who really wants your power, than arguing about a government mandated contract with a U.S. utility that has a 35% reserve margin.

He offered a deceptively simple answer to the question of why entrepreneurial outside managers, American or other, could do a better job of generating electricity than traditional utility monopolies. It was essentially a matter of increasing a power plant's availability, he said—the percentage of time during which the plant is actually pumping out usable electricity in relation to its technical capacity. A typical power plant operated by a utility in the United States might achieve 80 to 85 percent availability. In countries where state-owned utilities were even more tightly regulated on rates and investments, often seeming to serve the government of the day as patronage employment bureaus, availability would be much, much less.

Sant argued:

[Independent power producers] are normally paid more if their plants run better, while utilities are not. The added profit incentive is a powerful motivation to perform preventive maintenance, reduce outages and operate plants more efficiently—all of which can significantly increase a plant's availability.

Box 8.1

1993 letter to shareholders from Roger Sant and Dennis Bakke discussing the forces driving the emergence of International Electricity: Simple answers lack depth and universal applicability, but there do seem to be discernible themes in all the countries where we have had a serious interest.

- "Command and control" or "top down" or "socialist" methods of organizing an economy, where markets function poorly or not at all and where central governments own and operate the bulk of the productive assets, are in general disrepute, and for good reason. As countries change these practices, entrepreneurs develop, growth accelerates, and with it comes more demand for all types of infrastructure, including power (except in countries where top down methods created more infrastructure than was needed).

- Money is limited. Many governments now are choosing to allow foreign investment and participation in the power generation area because of both general public funds limitations and the enormous capital consuming nature of these facilities. And, in truth, a power plant in "foreign" hands is less of an affront to national sovereignty and security, it seems, than some other infrastructure investments. As an aside we note that the World Bank has led the way in urging reform and privatization of emerging market utility systems, and has tied these policy changes to the carrot and stick of funding. This has been very helpful.

- Existing systems run less than optimally. In some cases it would make more sense to sell off all the pieces and then watch market-driven owners take plant availabilities up ten or fifteen percentage points. This would alleviate a source of some "shortages" in electric systems. And this is what Argentina and Northern Ireland did in its purest form. Most other jurisdictions haven't quite been able to change the old, time-honored power generation paradigm sufficiently, overcome the union problems, or the concern about selling the national patrimony too cheaply, that stand in the way of this approach.

We are not trying here to make global policy. In fact, one thing we realized early on was our inability to really influence the legal and regulatory structure in a foreign location. If the country isn't ready for independent private power, we'll go elsewhere. But if they're selling power plants we're a buyer, and if they need electricity we're a provider.

Globalization will continue to test our mettle. . . . The days when we struggled with how to become more diverse are waning. Diversity, with all its richness and challenges, is upon us. How we make the most of the wonderful opportunities this affords us is the question. Will we do a good job choosing new partners and strengthening the relationships with those we have? Can we sort out how to live up to our social responsibility commitment in the new countries that we are starting to call home?

From the start of its international expansion, AES chose to recruit and employ local people at all levels of operation. An early policy statement declared that the company "does not believe that a largely expatriate staff is either appropriate or, in the long term, affordable for its operations." By 1994, United States citizens were no longer the majority within AES. A tabulation three years later revealed that English was the first language of no more than 8 percent of the company's people.

The returns of 1995 showed a learning curve erupting into a growth spurt. AES owned or controlled nineteen power plants in six countries, with a "presence" seeking out new business in thirty-five more. Total assets (hard assets, not trading contracts, which later became so troublesome for competitors such as Enron) grew from $1.7 billion in 1993 to $2.3 billion in 1995. Worldwide, "AES people" numbered 1,258. Three-quarters of the business development budget and personnel were committed to scouting opportunities in developing countries; AES projected that by the year 2000 at least half of the company's net income would come from outside the United States. Already in the pioneering Northern Ireland generating plants, savings in the cost per unit of electric output were as much as 20 percent; the workforce had been reduced by more than half.

In anticipation of international expansion and the need for working capital to help it compete with rival companies, AES acknowledged early in 1994 that its stock would be a normal growth stock after all, reversing the company policy of paying out substantially all its earnings in cash dividends. (To shareholders Sant and Bakke wrote: "We apologize to you all for our arrogance in thinking we could do that and still carry out our purpose of meeting electricity needs around the globe.") AES raised $69 million in 1993 by selling new shares to the public and subsequently split its common stock, three for two, in February 1994. (There were two subsequent splits, both two for one, in August 1997 and June 2000.)

Net income per share (adjusted for splits) rose from $0.24 in 1993 to $0.35 in 1995. From 1993 to 1995, AES common stock fluctuated between just under $4.00 and $6.00 per share, first trading on NASDAQ and then graduating to the New York Stock Exchange in 1996. After adjusting for splits, its share price at the initial public offering of June 1991 was $3.07. Adjusting further back to the start-up in 1982, the initial private investors had seen their investment multiply 480 times—from $0.0125 to $6.00 per share.

In 1996, AES' fifteenth year in operation, the growth spurt took over; the company had thirty-five power plants (including nine under construction) in eight countries: Argentina, Brazil, Pakistan, Hungary, Kazakhstan, China, the United States, and Britain. Total reported assets reached $3.6 billion. Net income (adjusted for splits) was $0.41 per share. The split adjusted price of common stock that year went from a low of $5.25, just below its 1995 peak, to a high on the New York Stock Exchange of just over $12.50. The actual AES payroll reached almost 6,000, but 7,000 more were on the job in power plants and related businesses managed by AES and acquired in partnerships without controlling equity.

The international industry of electricity in the 1990s was becoming quite different from what Sant and Bakke had envisaged when they launched their little start-up in the United States. Their business, as they had planned it, was to raise the capital (they had nothing serious of their own) to build sophisticated new electric power plants and then to operate them along the lines of their own management philosophy. By contrast, the electricity business that emerged in the 1990s involved not so much building better power plants as taking over existing facilities and making them work better. The entrepreneurship, in the words of energy consultant Anthony Churchill, was "about putting deals together, not building power plants."

Roger Sant, of course, was no slouch in doing deals: in broad-brush terms, that had been his calling long before he encountered deregulation, cogeneration, or electricity itself. It was those creative skills that enabled him and his teams to put together, against all odds, the financing packages for power plants at Deepwater, Beaver Valley, Shady Point, Thames, and Hawaii, all of which continued for years to come to function efficiently for the AES bottom line amid the dynamism of global expansion.

State-of-the-art power stations and the related infrastructure offer environmental advantages over the old plants, and they did indeed reduce the wholesale cost of electricity significantly. But in financial terms, as Churchill, a twenty-nine-year veteran of the World Bank, argued, "adding new capacity is part of a low-profit, commodity business." This became troublesome as the independent power producers began to expand their business overseas. "They are doing this at considerable risk and expect to be compensated for those risks," Churchill went on. "Owning and running a power plant for 30 years will not provide the appropriate compensation for this type of risk capital."

AES nonetheless set out to find opportunities for appropriate compensation. The company found that better returns might come at the other end of the power supply chain, in the distribution of electricity to the final consumers. Because distribution service remains a natural monopoly, the regulated revenue streams should provide a more dependable source of cash flow.

American utilities and power producers initially took a dim view of the distribution function in overseas markets, particularly in developing countries, where potential investors assumed that American firms could not assemble quickly enough the on-the-ground knowledge of local conditions. "Poor collection records and traditions of theft and other abuses all contribute to this generally negative perception," stated the *Electricity Journal* in 1995, laying out the case for investment in the distribution of electricity as well as its generation.

In many countries the distribution services have been allowed to deteriorate and often have received less attention and less investment than the more glamorous building of new plants. But this neglect also represents an opportunity. Much of what needs to be done is in the area of management, maintenance, and labor and customer relations. . . .

Most governments would welcome arrangements in which an investor group, preferably with a strong local partner, took over the distribution company for a modest up-front payment, but with a promise of future investments designed to meet the anticipated expansion of the market. Labor problems become less of an issue in rapidly expanding markets—in some distribution areas demand growth is over 20 percent per year.

Furthermore, for AES the provision of efficient and reliable electricity to a developing economy fit in with the company's declared commitment to social responsibility.

Tom Tribone recalled, following his move to Brazil after closing the pioneering generating project in Argentina, standing atop the hills outside Rio de Janeiro, looking down at the lights dotting the city streets, and saying to himself, "Look at all those customers!"

Brazil in the mid-1990s appeared poised, finally, to begin realizing its potential for industrial and social growth. So held the "Washington consensus." Prospects for political stability looked promising; ruinous inflation, endemic across Latin America, seemed under control. AES was but one of the newly dynamic international electric companies to move in, alongside competitors such as Enron and the El Paso Electric Company of the United States, Tractebel of Belgium, and Electricité de France (EDF). By this time, their sights were not limited to power-generating plants; they were ready to play in the distribution business as well.

AES was not accustomed to thinking of retail customers, the dotted lights of Rio's streets that had so moved Tom Tribone. After doing some significant spadework to line up investment partners, Tribone cornered Sant and Bakke on his next trip to Arlington and laid out the figures for acquiring a position in the business of distributing electricity to Rio de Janeiro. "What do you think?" he asked. AES was still operating like a family business, and the little cohort of officers around Sant's and Bakke's open offices decided that to make a bid, it would not be necessary to go to the board of directors for approval or even "advice." "We just went for it—the three of us," was how Sant remembered the decision to get the process started. "Time was short."

In May 1996, an international consortium led by AES won the bid to acquire a 50.44 percent controlling interest in Light Serviços de Eletricidade, one of Brazil's largest utilities, serving more than 2.7 million retail customers in Rio. The privatization package amounted to $1.7 billion; AES' share was just under $400 million.

This was nonetheless "our biggest equity investment ever," Sant and Bakke told investors, and "expanded our business for the first time into the distribution of electricity." "By its purchase of a major share in Rio Light in Brazil," wrote analyst Anthony Churchill, "AES was able to shift from a company that only built new plants to a broader based strategic investor."

Within two years, Light had acquired a controlling share of Eletropaulo Metropolitana Eletricidade de São Paulo, the biggest electric distribution company in Latin America. AES and EDF worked out a complex exchange of interests—buying out their other partners and assuming outstanding debts to Brazil's state development bank, Banco Nacional de Desenvolvimento Econômico e Social (BNDES)—leaving EDF in control of Light and AES in control of Eletropaulo. For the AES bottom line, the maneuver was equivalent to the purchase of South America's largest electric distributor for $1.8 billion, financed by a loan of $1.2 billion from BNDES—a long-term liability that would grow ever more troublesome in the coming years.

From 1995 to 2000, AES' power generation grew sevenfold; company shares on the New York Stock Exchange rose by 1,104 percent, reported the *Wall Street Journal*. (The Dow Jones electric utility index, by contrast, rose by just 57 percent in this period.) In September 1998, AES was added to the benchmark Standard & Poor's 500 Index, increasing its attractiveness to investors. "I woke up one morning and suddenly we were part of the index,"

Sant told the *Washington Post*. Years before, Sant had casually inquired whether AES met the index's criteria, but nothing further happened. "We're such a non-household word," he said. "We're probably the least well known company of our size. Fortunately, people who matter to our business know about us." One industry analyst concluded, "The places they go are perceived to be risky, but the way they structure their business deals is not."

The AES portfolio of electricity assets, operating in twenty-four countries by 2000, was still weighted toward the company's primary interest, power generation. It had acquired 15 local distribution companies, but this new activity seemed modest compared with more than 140 power plants under management on four continents. (Of these, North American plants recorded a capacity of 7,740 megawatts, but those in South America were double the size, at 15,231 megawatts. Plants in Asia, mainly China, totaled 11,713 megawatts; those in Europe, 7,449 megawatts, about the same as in North America.) Yet compared with the 140 power plants, those 15 distribution businesses provided no less than 40 percent of AES' revenues.

Snapshots of the AES management style and portfolio at the turn of the twenty-first century:

Hungary. In the economic transformation following the fall of communism, 49 percent of Hungary's state-owned electric utility was offered for privatization, with German, Swiss, and Austrian firms considered the likely buyers. Not naïve in the ways of capitalism, the new Hungarian planners offered state assets in packages—containing some that would be attractive and some that would be less so—in hopes of attracting high bids. In August 1996, AES acquired a controlling interest in three Soviet-era power plants ripe for modernization for $127 million, becoming the generator of about 20 percent of Hungary's electricity. But also in the package was an underground coal mine, not the sort of enterprise envisaged in the Sant-Bakke business plan. Nonetheless, under AES management the 1,271-person Lyukobanya mine came to operate at safety levels 40 percent better than at similar coal mines in the United States.

Georgia (the former Soviet Union). In October 1998, AES bought a 75 percent interest in the electric distribution company for Tbilisi, the national capital. On a subsequent visit to Washington, Georgia's president, Eduard Shevardnadze, asked to meet with Sant and Bakke to express his gratitude to AES for keeping electric power flowing throughout his capital without interruption for the first winter in his memory.

Kazakhstan (the former Soviet Union). AES acquired the 4,000-megawatt Ekibastuz coal-burning plant, one of the world's largest, in northern Kazakhstan. Just sixteen years old, it was already in dreary condition; of the total capacity, only 250 megawatts could be delivered. "I'd never seen anything more pitiful or more sickening," Sant said after examining the plant as chairman of the AES board, "to see how the Soviets took good engineering and botched the job." The turbines were in bad shape, part of the roof was falling in, and the smokestack was crooked. This acquisition was one decision that Mark Fitzpatrick, the AES group manager in Europe, did not want to make on his own. He submitted the purchase and retrofit plan to the AES board, which concurred that it was a long shot but a chance worth taking. AES invested $90 million just to bring the plant up to 25 percent of capacity and then bought five more generation and distribution businesses, for a total investment of $200 million. In 1999, Ekibastuz completed a million working hours without an accident that required anyone to miss even one day of work. AES controlled about 30 percent of Kazakhstan's electricity-generating capacity.

"It's a very tough operating environment," said Vitaly Lee, a Kazakh national who became the AES country director, "considering the low income of the general population and the regulators' desire to keep the rates low and ignore the needs of the company to invest in upgrading." When cash payments for electricity provided were not forthcoming, the AES people in the plants bartered for eggs, vodka, even cars—dodging constant demands for bribes. "I think Kazakhstan wants us, though it is not always easy to tell," Bakke told a *New York Times* correspondent. "Business can be risky everywhere."

Pakistan. AES started developing two power plants in Pakistan in 1995 under the leadership of an imaginative young American, J. Stuart Ryan.

"These plants will be our largest single operating unit with the highest potential economic impact on the company," Bakke reported. Within a few years, the PakGen and Lal Pir plants were ranked the most successful AES ventures in the developing world. "To develop, in a highly disciplined manner, a much needed and affordable power complex in a country as poor as Pakistan, was and is tremendously satisfying," Sant concluded, reminiscing about his years of company leadership. Some three hundred AES people convened at Lahore in October 2000 for their semi-annual business review meeting, followed by a dinner in their honor given by President Pervez Musharraf.

India. As early as 1992, AES had started exploring the Indian market for electricity, one of the world's four largest. (The installed electricity capacity in India was only 90 megawatts per million people; in the United States it was 3,000 megawatts.) Over the ensuing years, AES acquired three businesses in the rural state of Orissa, two distribution companies, and prospects for a greenfield generation plant in the Ib Valley, which languished on the drawing board under a morass of red tape and bureaucratic obstruction. As in Kazakhstan, nonpayment of electric bills and illegal tapping into transmission wires seemed somehow normal; according to one estimate, 10 to 20 percent of generated electricity was never paid for.

Uganda. With encouragement from the World Bank and regional development banks, AES embarked on an ambitious project to build a hundred-foot-high concrete dam for 200–250 megawatts of hydroelectric power generation at Bujagali Falls, near the point where the Nile River turns north. Less than 5 percent of Uganda's population had access to electricity; candles and lanterns were the routine power source.

What had seemed a straightforward development project, however, encountered an unexpected complication. The Basoga and Baganda peoples living by Bujagali Falls believe that their revered ancestors inhabit the waters of the Nile. An AES environmental impact report concluded that "the dwelling places of a number of spirits will require relocation either before construction commences or before the reservoir area is inundated. . . . No site can be destroyed or damaged until the necessary ceremonies or rituals have been carried out."

AES hired a local specialist in traditional religions to oversee the proper procedures, and the company offered to build new homes for 400 families willing to relocate. "In terms of consultation, resettlement and compensation, they have gone well beyond the minimal guidelines," an expert from the Worldwide Fund for Nature told the *Financial Times*. The newspaper went on to comment, "The way AES has kept opposition to a minimum may provide a useful primer for other companies."

Britain. In 1999, in the course of restructuring the electricity generation industry, National Power, the former British government monopoly, offered for privatization the giant 4,065-megawatt coal-fired Drax Power Station in the north of England. Drax was considered the largest and cleanest coal-burning power plant in Europe, and it could command a high price—perhaps $3 billion. The AES business development man on the spot was a young Englishman, John Turner, with no more than eight months' experience in the company; Sant and Bakke had not yet even met him. AES people were not shy in those buoyant times, and Turner made bold to put together a proposal and submit it to the board and senior officers for "advice." Directors and officers submitted ideas to the man in the field, in effect authorizing him to make a bid if he thought it worthwhile. He did, and his AES bid was accepted.

The key to Turner's plan was a long-term purchase contract for half the Drax output with Texas Utilities Europe, a subsidiary of the TXU Corporation, which had already invested more than $10 billion in the international, mainly British, electricity marketplace. The other half of the giant plant's output would be available for the British spot market, which showed no signs of weakening prices. The AES board shared Turner's confidence that this was an adequate hedge.

Within two years, the perfect hedge became the perfect failure. Competition from new plants coming online pulled down British spot market prices by more than 40 percent. And on the other side, facing its own liquidity problem, TXU abandoned its European subsidiary, leaving the mighty Drax plant with neither its primary customer nor its sustaining hedge.

The conventional skepticism within International Electricity was that investment in developing countries, which might lack the discipline of a mature marketplace, carried a high risk of default and collapse. In the AES experience, the most unsettling financial default came not in a "backward" country but in Great Britain. Failing to find a workable restructuring after many tries, AES had to turn the project over to its lenders and let a major commitment in the developed Western world fall from its portfolio.

In anticipation of building a portfolio this diverse and adventurous, Bakke had sent a reflective memo to AES people early in 1995 sharing discussions that had been going on in the Arlington offices about adding a tagline to the company name: "AES Corporation, the Global Power Company." "We think this does a better job of capturing the essence of AES," the new chief executive wrote. "It reflects the shift of resources, people and need for our services outside the U.S. It also hints at the aggressiveness with which we would like to attack electricity needs around the world."

Box 8.2

1995 AES Annual Report by Dennis Bakke

The array of needs for what AES has to offer, and the challenges and opportunities those needs present, are so diverse, complicated and dynamic, that any attempt to have a centralized strategic plan or process is futile.

- In some places we will emphasize greenfield plants, in others acquisitions.
- In some places the plants may have pipeline or transmission lines attached to them and in others the facilities may be small units.
- Partners may be the way to go in China, but not necessarily the right approach in other countries.
- Project financing is best in many places, but can't be done in others.
- Long-term contracts are the goal in certain situations and short-term ones in others.
- In many cases we use our assets primarily to generate electricity; in others we may use them primarily as a hedge against selling electricity through power marketing.

But then he added a cautionary note, prophetic in light of the stresses that came to mark his coming tenure of company leadership. Bakke warned against the temptations of "careless" decision making, saying, "Thinking globally, and thinking big, will require doubling our scrutiny and analyses." The AES story of the coming six years would reveal what scant measure of attention was paid to his warning.

A broad assembly of AES people gathered over ten days in October for a series of retreats and self-examination. A core group of ten responsible officers, including those present at the start-up fourteen years back, spent a long day at Sant's Virginia farm, reviewing the course of their company's growth, its focus and orientation, and, though they disliked the word, its strategy. Besides Sant and Bakke, the company at the Farm Meeting, as it was long remembered, consisted of Paul Hanrahan, Barry Sharp, Stu Ryan, Tom Tribone, John Ruggirello, Mark Fitzpatrick, Ken Woodcock, and Roger Naill. This inner circle was mindful, of course, of the passing of company leadership from Sant to Bakke, perceived to be proceeding with all the smoothness of the cofounders' long and intimate working relationship.

The self-image of "the Global Power Company" was uppermost in many minds. "It was magical how it transformed the way we did business," Sant said. "People reviewing decisions asked, 'If we're really trying to be the leading global power company, would we have done this or that?' . . . The company just exploded thereafter."

The October Farm Meeting reaffirmed both the diversity and the legitimacy of differing business strategies, Bakke concluded, and the importance of decentralizing strategy development. But it also confirmed the long-standing AES practice of seeking "advice," not "approval," from Arlington headquarters and colleagues across the company before making decisions in the field. This practice served not only to draw upon the collective experience but also, in Bakke's words, "to develop passionate supporters who care about and will hold us accountable for results."

"We reflected on some past AES mistakes and concluded that we make lots of them," Bakke wrote in his memorandum of the meeting.

There is basic agreement that some of our past mistakes might have been avoided if we were bigger at the time, or had a "global power company" attitude that would have used strength to overcome the pressures that pushed us toward decisions that turned out to be mistakes.

Most of us also believe that being bigger is helpful as we face the world competition. But there is also a strong majority that believes we are big now and growing fast enough to be able to meet future challenges. Most of our people believe that reputation is more crucial than size as a factor in success

This means there is little excitement for mergers or capital infusions to make us bigger quickly, that also carry with them additional risks to the ownership and culture we enjoy today.

Bakke found it "fascinating to find out that many of the learning conclusions we had come to shortly after making a particular mistake may very well become less relevant as the world changes." Thus, the discussions concluded with a "commitment to seek understanding from our mistakes," but not to "memorize 'the mistake lesson' with such a rigidity that action in new situations would be inhibited."

Grand strategy, or lack thereof, inevitably gave way to operational and financial matters in congenial give-and-take discussions that October. For example, recognizing new conditions presented by business activity in foreign countries, the AES leadership group agreed to offer the public in emerging countries, "as broadly-based as possible," equity shares in individual plants and projects "as a way to give local people an avenue to participate, and another way to mitigate the risk of expropriation or other hostile political action."

AES' internal compensation policy emerged as a thorny question, in particular the payment of significant bonuses upon the closing of new business deals. Several participants questioned the message sent by this emphasis on closing and not necessarily on subsequent performance. At this early stage in the company's expansion, no clear consensus emerged; the issue would become even more contentious in the dramatic growth years ahead.

Overall, the Farm Meeting of October 1995 set new directions for AES—within the culture and values of the past but under new executive leadership and with new opportunities for International Electricity. On one point there was no longer discussion or doubt: from its modest beginning just fourteen years before, in the minds of its people, AES was now indeed the Global Power Company.

NINE

Global Values

For the founding generation of AES, the dynamic growth of the late 1990s brought financial returns unimagined in the early years. Revenues grew by 41 percent annually over five years, and earnings per share grew by 18 percent yearly. In 1998 alone, AES raised about $6 billion in the capital markets; according to one calculation, only four other American public companies raised more private capital.

So far, so good. But to the loyalists within the company, their AES had always been grounded on something more fundamental than the balance sheets, however glowing those might be. The business success put to a profound test the value system that gave AES its proud sense of identity.

As early as 1993, with the global expansion scarcely under way, Roger Sant and Dennis Bakke had raised three basic issues for the AES faithful to consider:

1. Could the core values—in shorthand, fairness, integrity, social responsibility, and "fun"—become nothing more than worn-out creeds, no longer serving to drive and order the behavior of the company and the decisions made by its people?
2. Physical separation of offices and plants around the world might vastly complicate the collective application of the values, endangering

in particular the founders' conviction that AES people can and should hold one another accountable for living up to their shared beliefs.

3. Finally, would the company and its people be capable of defining and applying professed values in diverse cultures, among populations of differing faiths and social systems?

"Can we be AES in Kazakhstan or Hungary?" Sant wondered. If cultural differences between workers at the Thames power plant in Connecticut and Shady Point in rural Oklahoma had caused such anguish in 1992, how much more complex would be the nuances of cultures across continents? More than just a few skeptical AES people in the field complained about "great difficulty maintaining the values overseas. . . . If we cannot maintain our priority on values, we should not go overseas," came the argument.

A fundamental issue involved assigning priorities in the application of general values. Where was social responsibility: reducing emissions of carbon dioxide and sulfur dioxide, or improving community health and education among plant workers and families in the neighborhoods? On returning from Pakistan, where the adult literacy rate was less than 40 percent, even Sant had to argue, "You can't go to Pakistan and say that the number-one priority is global warming."

Developing countries often had less stringent environmental standards than industrialized countries, opening the temptation to construct or operate a plant in full compliance with local laws but "'dirtier' than those built in the U.S.," as a discussion in the *Electricity Journal* put it, only inviting "criticism from environmental groups, shareholders, and others at home." Public criticism aside, would this be the AES way?

Listening to the skeptics, Sant and Bakke nonetheless persisted in what was becoming an article of faith: the company's value system could be properly applied and survive wherever AES operated. Bakke took the lead in public statements:

Roger Naill and I share a smile in almost every location we visit together for the first time. Invariably, some person listening to our presentation on AES will make a comment something like, "These are wonderful ideas, but they won't work here." This is probably a variant of "These are nice *American* ideas." However, we also hear the same point in the U.S. and we have heard it almost every other place AES is trying to work.

Some global organizations solve this problem by adopting values and philosophies that are flexible. "When in Rome, do as the Romans do" is the operative approach. At AES we are trying an almost opposite way of living. We hold tightly to a central purpose as to why the company exists. . . . While we don't know for sure that the AES approach will work in every location around the world, our experience thus far is that it probably can.

Early on, Sant and Bakke had launched what they called a "values survey," an annual questionnaire sent to all AES people for their assessment, anonymously for those more comfortable that way, of how well the company was living up to its declared values. Bakke would say that each year from October to December he spent most of his time as chief executive officer reading every single response, signed and unsigned. The results became the lead topic in annual reports alongside, sometimes ahead of, the financial data.

Although it only confirmed his own hunches, Bakke continued to marvel at the similarity in assessments—both positive and negative—from diverse people in far-flung locations. "Two or three years after a business becomes part of AES," he argued, an outside reader of a typical assessment "would find it difficult to detect from what part of the world it had originated."

"These are basic Islamic values," was one response that Bakke particularly liked; or "I'm free to develop myself—I feel I can reach the moon." To be fair, he would also quote some of the negatives from the field: "Understanding is much easier than putting into practice." And in the AES spirit of fun, he could not resist relaying a complaint that the values survey was just "a giant social experiment for Bakke!" One later (and anonymous) comment from within AES contained a sobering message: "AES's culture is a really good concept run amok—people use culture as an excuse."

The core of the challenge to AES' culture—and indeed to its survival in the next few years—was the swelling number of workers within the company, with the acquisitions of fully staffed plants and businesses. In 1996, some 90 percent of the ten thousand or so AES people had come aboard in the previous two years. "People were acquired, not hired," Sant said long afterward. "Perhaps we were too ready to believe that anyone could be quickly converted to being a fully capable AES person." But Bakke stuck to plan, citing, for example, the company's evolving experience in post-Soviet Kazakhstan:

> Our team has done an incredible job of explaining to the government that capitalism doesn't have to be "gangsterism," which is how some of the people there perceive it. Our people have been able to demonstrate to the government and to the people working in the plants we have acquired what AES is all about—how we do business and how we represent a different version of capitalism.
>
> And these are people who haven't worked at AES for all that long. Some of them have only been with us six months, but they get the values, and they improve on them.

In acquired installations overseas, as well as in America, a specific matter became a much-discussed issue in the evolving company culture: the distinction between salaried compensation and hourly pay, the latter of which was the norm in industrial facilities. Decades before, Thomas J. Watson of IBM had pioneered reform in the psychology underlying the issues; Sant and Bakke put it into practice, offering all AES people the choice of which way to be paid.

"What are you saying when you pay someone an hourly wage?" Sant asked a *Harvard Business Review* editor.

> You're saying, "We only care about the physical time you spend in the plant. We don't trust you, so you have to punch a time clock." That attitude is left over from the Industrial Revolution, and that's not the way we feel.
>
> When you pay someone a salary and make them eligible for bonuses and stock ownership, you are saying, "Our assumptions about you are no different from those we have about the plant leader. You can and should bring your brainpower and soul—your whole person—to work." . . .

About 50 percent of our workers who used to get paid by the hour have converted themselves to salary, and we hope that close to 100 percent will choose that approach eventually. Generally, once people try it, they love it. . . . They see themselves differently.

The new compensation alternative was "not a cost-saving move," Sant and Bakke emphasized:

Total compensation paid to these individuals in salary, bonuses and stock options is on average likely to be higher than under the old system. . . . This new system emphasizes compensation for what a person accomplishes, rather than how many hours he or she is in attendance. . . . People are encouraged to work smarter, not longer.

Bakke paid a visit to the modernizing Tisza II plant in Hungary, where workers accustomed to communist-era employment had been arguing for three months about the new compensation alternative. Over ninety minutes, Bakke listened to the conflicting views from the plant floor and then argued his own. At the end, as Bakke reported the incident, a worker named Attila Legoza tentatively approached the head of the company from America:

Through an interpreter he asked if his contract converting to "all salary" could be signed on the spot by the visitor. Within minutes, dozens of others had run to their lockers and returned with contracts for signature.

For many in attendance, it felt like the Berlin Wall of industrial labor/management structure was crumbling before their eyes. In this emotional impromptu ceremony, one more barrier to a fun workplace was disappearing.

Disruption of labor-management traditions, whether in communist or capitalist societies, was nothing new for Sant and Bakke. The issue had raised its contentious head in the earliest years of AES. The second power plant their company built, Beaver Valley in Pennsylvania, had an existing, if skeletal, workforce in place, and inevitably the time came to renew the labor contract. In the time-honored pattern, the workers, through their union, would present a list of demands, and management would come up with an equally formidable list. The two sides would argue, negotiate, and settle. That was the way it had always been done.

At Beaver Valley, the plant manager, John Ruggirello (who later became a senior vice president of AES), decided to do things differently—without, of course, bothering to ask anyone at company headquarters. Bob Waterman, management consultant and AES board member, described what happened next in a 1994 book called *What America Does Right*:

> Union leadership presented its long list and asked management for theirs. Ruggirello broke the mold. "We don't have one," he said. "What do you mean, 'you don't have one'?" asked the astonished union boss. Ruggirello reiterated, "We don't have a list. You figure out which of the items on the list are truly important to you, which are in our mutual best interest, and which are fair. Then get back to us and we'll probably go along."

Plant manager Ruggirello, and Sant and Bakke's AES, did just that. An agreement satisfactory to both sides emerged without any of the acrimony of a prolonged bargaining.

At another of the acquired plants, AES Redondo Beach in California, unionized workers voted to decertify their union. Bakke insisted that AES was not against labor unions—"We work with many of them around the world." But he said that the Redondo Beach workforce "realized that the AES philosophy of radically decentralized decision making puts them in control and effectively eliminates 'management.' Without a management to confront and with no one designated as 'labor,' these people did not see a substantial role for their union."

That sort of attitude could have taken hold when the company was small, when workers on the plant floors had genuine contact with the company leaders at headquarters. However, once AES started acquiring operating companies around the world, at the same time acquiring thousands of employees ("people"), the labor-management relationship became more troublesome for the new owners' value systems. Few of the new people had more than a handshake acquaintance with the founders in far-off Arlington, and most were certainly not accustomed to the company's unusual management style.

Job protection is invariably an early issue whenever some entrepreneurial foreign management takes over. Bloated payrolls, after all, were among the offenses that privatization had been designed to cure. From Northern Ireland to India, the likelihood of staff reductions became perceived as the dark side of the AES culture. Sant and Bakke minced no words in their joint annual letter of 1996:

> Most of the businesses we have acquired over the past two years came to us with far too many people. It is impossible to create a workplace environment where people can maximize their learning and use skills effectively when there are excessive numbers of people. Everyone becomes underemployed.

At plant after plant, AES introduced job training opportunities and voluntary severance programs, with loans to help workers who left to establish their own businesses. Bakke described a typical encounter:

> On my last trip to our recently acquired generation business in India, the first question I got from nervous folks at the plant was, "Are we going to lose our jobs?" Diplomatically, I said "Yes, every person here will lose their job." That got their attention. . . .
>
> Over time none of us has the job we had before. . . . We accelerate the losing of one's current job by requiring people to broaden their responsibilities, to cross train, to be held accountable. . . . Even one extra person will reduce the responsibility level of others in the organization.

In 1998, the *Harvard Business Review*, respected journal of Sant's and Bakke's alma mater, published an article spectacularly debunking the notion of "worker empowerment," then fashionable as a panacea for responsible corporate governance. The name of the author attracted as much notice as the topic: Chris Argyris, a professor emeritus at Harvard Business School and an acknowledged dean of academic management theorists—not a personage to be dismissed.

"Empowerment: The Emperor's New Clothes" was the headline. "Managers love empowerment in theory, but the command-and-control model is what they trust and know best," Argyris explained. "For their part, employees are often ambivalent about empowerment—it is great as long as they are not held personally responsible."

In other words, management didn't mean what it said about "empowerment," and workers, coming right down to it, didn't want it. Argyris argued that, on hearing these words from the boss, "employees interpret these messages as 'do your own thing—the way we tell you.'"

Argyris never mentioned AES by name, and much of his depiction of aggregate corporate behavior did not apply to the company. But Sant and Bakke had become prominent figures in corporate governance theory, champions of the novel style in labor-management relations that Argyris had debunked. Moreover, their enterprise was riding high on the charts of growth companies. Early in 1999, the *Harvard Business Review* followed up Argyris' broadside with Sant and Bakke's contrary view.

Both Sant and Bakke had misgivings about the word "empowerment." "We knew that we wanted to create a very different kind of company, that's for sure," Bakke said. "I don't think we'd used the word 'empowerment'— I'm not sure it was even around in 1981." But, he went on: "Everything about how we organize gives people the power and the responsibility to make important decisions. . . . The AES system is designed to make sure power gets distributed throughout the organization."

Sant went along with "empowerment" for the sake of the dialogue. But afterward he wondered whether he should have been more precise. "'Empowerment' was never the core of our business model," he said, thinking back on the *Review* interview.

The whole notion of giving more power to more people, or the giving up power by senior leadership, was never regarded as a virtue in itself. It was much more an outcome of our value of having fun in the job. Just making fun one of our core values caused us to try to create an environment where people enjoyed what they did. Empowerment, as it has become known, or the giving up of power and responsibility as we described it then, seemed to be an essential part of a fun working environment.

Our system starts with a lack of hierarchy. . . . The more authority figures you have above you, the more likely it is that you won't make decisions yourself. . . . We want people to take ownership of the whole—the way you care about your house. You run it, you keep it up, you fix it.

What about expertise? Specialized training and experience in a particular craft? Bakke had often characterized specialization as "the root of a lot of boredom." Wouldn't the absence of specialization interfere with a company's efficiency? "It might," Sant conceded. "But we try to reinvent the wheel every time we get a chance. The process of learning and doing is what creates engagement—fun."

In conclusion, probing beyond the theme of empowerment, the *Review* editor, Suzy Wetlaufer, posed a fundamental question to the two founders: "You both believe businesses should benefit society. Why?"

This was a question that had grown into an unspoken commonplace over the eighteen years of the Sant-Bakke partnership. The responses in 1999 were candid and more revealing, perhaps, than intended.

"Dennis and I actually come from somewhat different places on this one," Sant began.

My original notions about social responsibility arose because I had seen a lot of environmental irresponsibility. . . . I came to believe that people couldn't keep doing unsustainable things. . . . There had to be some answers to the question, How can we create a society that would stop stealing from the capital of the planet? And I realized that business played an important role.

Companies could handle social responsibility in an integrative way, not tack it on at the end of their thinking about operations, like some kind of afterthought. That is, business could build social responsibility into its values and practices. . . . We want our company to do everything it can to be a responsible part of our communities—proactively, not reactively.

Then Bakke came in with his own, somewhat different statement of motivation:

> My belief in empowerment comes from my Christian faith, but many of my beliefs are not inconsistent with the fundamentals of Buddhism, Judaism, and Islam. . . .
>
> Personally, I start with the book of Genesis, which tells us that we are put on earth to glorify God by stewarding our resources for ourselves and for others. Our nonhierarchical structure and our desire to engage the wholeness of people comes from my belief that God created each one of us in his image. The Bible teaches that each person is holy, special, and unique. We are creative, accountable, trustworthy—and fallible. . . .
>
> Social responsibility comes from a requirement to love our neighbor as ourselves. Treat each person with respect and dignity. In essence, I would love to get the workplace as close to the Garden as possible, knowing we can't. But I shouldn't stop trying.

The interview published in the *Harvard Business Review* turned out to be the last joint statement offered by the cofounders of AES. For their 1999 annual report, Sant withheld his name from the traditional letter to shareholders and friends, which had been a fixture from the company's formation.

"Even though I love the partnership evidenced by a joint letter," he wrote in a separate letter from the chairman, "it seems less than honest to continue the practice." For, as he declined to admit at the time (but would later), Roger Sant was having increasing difficulty with the way his partner, Dennis Bakke, was managing their company.

By this time Sant, as chairman of the AES board, was spending no more than one day a week at AES as he pursued his own environmental interests: the World Wildlife Fund, where he was also chairman; his and his wife's Summit Foundation; and a dozen or so other not-for-profit organizations supporting programs from Mesoamerica to the Anacostia River in southeast Washington, DC. He traveled frequently to Brazil, not to check on languishing AES business ventures but to promote campaigns for protecting biodiversity in Amazonia and the Atlantic Forest. To his mind, the least welcome contribution a retired chief executive officer could make would be to second-guess the direction of his successor, a longtime protégé and partner.

Argyris had made a concluding point in his broadside against empowerment, as he saw it. "Calculate factors such as morale, satisfaction, and even commitment into your human relations policies, but do not make them the ultimate criteria. They are penultimate. The ultimate goal is performance."

Sant and Bakke were at one in rejecting part of Argyris' conclusion, that individuals can "report low morale" and still be excellent performers—at least, that was not the kind of company they wanted to run. But Sant reluctantly came to appreciate the more basic point. Argyris had warned:

> When morale, satisfaction, and sense of empowerment are used as the ultimate criteria for success in organizations, they cover up many of the problems that organizations must overcome in the 21st century.

The twenty-first century was not two years old when that lesson burst into full view at AES.

TEN

Implosion

As Roger Sant and Dennis Bakke were explaining their values-driven management model in the pages of the *Harvard Business Review*, two academic business analysts, Charles A. O'Reilly and Jeffrey Pfeffer of Stanford University, were completing a book called *Hidden Value: How Great Companies Achieve Extraordinary Results with Ordinary People*. AES was one of their prime studies—not surprising, considering the wide notice the company was attracting. But a note of caution intruded on their otherwise upbeat portrayal; their seventh chapter was titled "AES: Is This Global Company Out of Control?"

"Control" as such was never uppermost, of course, in the AES value system. As Sant himself would say, his was a company that just "assumed that their people are good, that you don't need to control them, that you can depend on them." But the two professors were addressing a hard-nosed financial community, and the thesis of their book required a note of reassurance. Everyone at AES, they concluded, "has decisions to make and has accountability for his or her actions and decisions. . . . The company has built a strong system of mutual control, . . . a system that truly unleashes their ideas and their energies." Although O'Reilly and Pfeffer's point was arguably valid for the years of their research, a stern test of their conclusion was developing as they went to press, with implications largely unnoticed even within AES itself.

In 1996, after declaring itself "the Global Power Company," AES, under Bakke's leadership, tacitly altered two basic features of the founding business strategy:

1. The number of new operating projects each year increased dramatically.
2. The strategy of nonrecourse financing (i.e., each power plant or business standing on its own financially, without creditors' recourse to the parent company) was relaxed. Ever larger amounts of corporate funds were committed to finance growth.

From the late 1980s through 1995, AES' growth was marked by one new power plant or project coming online each year (except in 1992, when business growth actually doubled, to two). Starting in 1996, seven, eight, or nine new AES projects became operational each year, almost all of them acquisitions of existing facilities rather than newly designed greenfield plants. And the up-front corporate investment, which had never amounted to more than $100 million in any year, became $572 million in 1996 and rose to more than $4.5 billion in 2000.

In the buoyant enthusiasm of the new era of International Electricity, the goal of business was to make the deal, for its immediate effect on the growth curve. Only unimaginative drones would pay much attention to how efficiently and profitably the project turned out after the deal was closed. One disgruntled investor complained to AES consultants a couple of years later that "AES doesn't have a strategy—they just throw money at people and tell them to be creative."

When consultants and analysts independent of top management examined the records of the boom years—the company's actual operations, as opposed to the exciting prospects—they came to sobering conclusions. Far from reflecting anticipated, or even reasonable, profits, the effective returns over the company's cost of capital were *negative* in 1997, and in 1999 there was an aggregate loss of nearly 4 percent. "We recognize that optimism is a necessary ingredient in entrepreneurship," wrote one investment analyst, but company management "tends not to recognize reality until it hits them in the head."

At AES, management was not alone in neglecting to notice the financial metrics of the growth plan in real time. At the start of 2000, nothing seemed to disturb an uninterrupted horizon of ever more growth—and with more growth would come more profit, right?

In the volatile ways of commodities, prospects for the United States electricity industry were turning upward again, when for a decade only the world overseas had offered growth potential. Particularly enticing was the rich and newly deregulated electricity market of California.

As 2000 began, AES completed an acquisition from Southern California Edison of three gas-fueled power plants in the Los Angeles area, at Redondo Beach, Alamitos, and Huntington Beach. All provided good opportunities for upgrading to meet efficiency and environmental standards—just what AES wanted to do, and had demonstrated in its start-up years it was good at doing in a competitive, free-market system. Of the total cost of $786 million, AES secured about 90 percent financing from a group led by Credit Suisse First Boston.

Central to the financing package, in the long-standing AES model, were long-term contracts for supplying fuel and then, in turn, long-term contracts for selling the electricity, so-called tolling arrangements. As long as the plants operated well, prices for both sides were essentially defined for twenty years ahead, providing stability of costs and earnings. The special twist for the three Los Angeles power stations, called the Southland plants, was that the fuel supplier and the electricity customer were the same: the Williams Companies. "Williams gives us natural gas and we convert it to kilowatt-hours," Sant explained. "Then they take the kilowatt-hours back and sell them. It's not a formal partnership. It's a contractual relationship." The model was conservative, deliberately surrendering upside potential, but in contrast to many of the new businesses in this period it fit AES' founding strategy of minimizing risk in an otherwise volatile industry.

Then, in May, AES announced the $667 million acquisition of a 56 percent interest in an 885-megawatt plant in Nevada called the Mohave Generating Station, a major power provider for Arizona, Nevada, and southern California. Unexpectedly and belatedly, the California Public Utilities

Commission (CPUC) blocked the deal, amid fears that a poorly conceived deregulation plan would shatter the California power market. AES tried to have the ruling reversed, without success.

With the onset of the summer of 2000, the CPUC's fears became reality: California's power system began to malfunction. Supply became short and unreliable; wholesale prices soared. Everyone in government and industry blamed everyone else in government and industry for a system of deregulation that was going amok.

AES, as one of the out-of-state generating companies, was a readily available scapegoat. As Bakke put it, AES was hit simultaneously by consumer groups in California, which demanded more electricity from the newly acquired power stations, and by the South Coast Air Quality Management District, which charged AES with operating the plants for more hours than allowed under its environmental permits. And as independent power-generating companies were accused of profiteering, AES, with its conservative long-term tolling contracts, was actually losing money in California.

California and Mohave notwithstanding, at the start of 2001 AES executives felt good about the company's overall portfolio and gave financial analysts the usual positive projections of higher earnings for the coming year, and continuing to 2005. A writer for *Business Week* later recalled the company telling analysts "to expect a five-year compounded annual earnings-per-share growth in the range of 25 to 30 percent."

Dazzled by such prospects, analysts and the investing public paid scant attention to a dark smudge on the portfolio: Brazil, where the national economy was deteriorating rapidly. And it was here that AES had made its largest investment. The country's network of hydroelectric generating plants found its fuel supply threatened by successive years of drought; investment funds for new plants were scarce. Eventually, electricity was rationed and consumption plunged, pulling down the anticipated returns from the distribution businesses. Given the stresses across the whole economy, the Brazilian currency, the real, fell from 1.96 to the dollar at the start of 2001 to 2.41. AES believed that its contracts would provide adjustment for a weakening currency but meanwhile received its revenues in reals while having to pay dollars to service its debts. When the expected adjustment did not come through, the company's Brazilian businesses were in the dangerous position of counting on diminishing soft-currency revenues to service hard-currency debt.

In California, the power shortages and high price volatility that had started in the summer of 2000 only worsened. State and federal power authorities began investigating the operations of the competitive electric companies, including AES, to determine whether they had manipulated the wildly fluctuating power markets to enhance their profits at the expense of California utilities and consumers. AES turned over reams of internal records to demonstrate that its 4,450 megawatts of generating capacity at its three Los Angeles plants was contracted under the tolling agreements at predetermined prices to its wholesale customer, the Williams Companies; AES thus could not share in the windfalls accruing to Williams, Enron, and other power-trading companies as the forward price of electricity soared.

Then the internal files turned up incidental recorded telephone conversations between the AES and Williams control rooms suggesting that the AES generating plants might be complicit in holding back their electric output in order to reap larger returns later on, from rising spot rates. Never mind that no increased profit would come to AES from holding back; in the growing atmosphere of suspicion regarding the California power market, it was easy to lump AES in with all the other companies.

Only gradually did the story as it actually played out become clearer. Early in the year, AES had filed formal notice of scheduled production interruptions in April and May 2000, pursuing a plan that had been made at acquisition, three months before, to upgrade the old Southland plants to meet the company's environmental and efficiency standards. Electric output, accordingly, would be reduced for days or even weeks at a time, on a schedule announced well in advance. On April 27, as forward prices were rising, a Williams technician told an AES counterpart, "If your Unit 4 outage runs long and if you need more time, we don't have a problem with that." In guarded banter, the Williams controller said that Williams, the customer, would not go so far as to give AES, the supplier, any cut of windfall profits, only a relaxation of the contracted schedule for delivering the power.

Later that day, a more senior AES employee called the Williams repre-
sentative to confirm his understanding that "you guys were saying that it
might not be such a bad thing if it took us a little while longer to do our
work?" The recorded reply was, "We're not trying to talk you into doing it
but it wouldn't hurt, you know, we wouldn't throw a fit if it took any longer."
"Then you wouldn't hit us for availability?" asked the AES officer. "I don't
want you to do something underhanded," replied the Williams representa-
tive, "but if there's work you can continue to do—" The AES officer interrupted, "I understand. You don't have to talk anymore."

A week or so later, two other Williams and AES technicians exchanged
gossip about various possible shutdown plans. A Williams employee said,
laughing, "That's weird." The AES technician responded, "Yeah, they're playing games."

Accusations of market manipulation and profiteering gained traction among
angry Californians and the broader community of electricity policy analysts.
Respected academic specialists at Harvard University and the Massachusetts
Institute of Technology, neighbors on the Charles River at Cambridge, reached
opposing conclusions in professional journals. On March 14, 2001, armed with
transcripts supplied by AES of these recorded exchanges the year before, the
Federal Energy Regulatory Commission (FERC) ordered Williams and AES to
explain why they had withheld power from the generating plants. Had either
company committed an abuse of market power?

The recorded conversations, however embarrassing, revealed no manipulation—only talk of "weird," "wild," and "kinda interesting" ideas. After AES' inves-
tigation of its own shop, Senior Vice President Ken Woodcock was able to state
flatly that "AES never engaged in illegal or improper behavior in this matter." Six
weeks later, FERC concluded its inquiry, deciding not to charge AES with market abuse. Future investigations at state and federal levels reached the same conclusions, absolving AES of any responsibility in market manipulation.

But Stuart Ryan, the up-and-coming vice president, who had just
returned from Singapore to oversee AES' California businesses, indulged in
cheerful sarcasm. "If we're going to be hit with all this political flak anyway, wouldn't it be nice if we were at least making money?" Sant, Waterman,

and other longtime directors hated quips like this; even in jest, they could be cited to undermine the AES value system.

The woes of California and Brazil notwithstanding, years of entrepreneurial effort by "the Global Power Company" bore fruit through most of 2001. With each passing month, AES business scouts around the world closed their deals at a rapidly increasing pace.

In February, AES announced the purchase of a 290-megawatt generating plant in Nigeria, situated on an offshore barge. (The seller was Enron of Houston, and the transaction became notorious in the coming year as an example of Enron's accounting machinations.)

In April, Ukraine announced the sale of its privatized distribution system for the capital city, Kiev. For $45.9 million AES acquired a 75 percent share, with the balance to be offered in shares to company employees and the Ukrainian public. Two weeks later, AES acquired a second Ukrainian electric distribution company; it was the only bidder.

May: Bakke went to Brazil and vented his frustration at the deterioration of AES' position. Saying, "Brazil has not been a good experience for AES," he announced suspension of a scheduled $2 billion investment in ten new power plants. Three days later, he was in Santiago to announce that AES would invest $1 billion in Chile's power industry over the coming five years. By the end of May, an AES team was completing the deal to develop two large power stations in southern Bulgaria.

June: AES expansion in South America (except Brazil) roared ahead. The trade press reported that AES planned to invest $1.256 billion in Venezuelan generation and distribution assets through 2005. AES now had operating interests in Argentina, Brazil, Chile, Colombia, the Dominican Republic, El Salvador, Mexico, and Venezuela. Between one-quarter and one-third of the company's total cash flow for 2001 was projected to come from the Latin American subsidiaries.

July: AES closed on a deal to buy the energy assets of a subsidiary of Thermo Electron Corporation for $238 million, gaining a first foothold in the electricity markets of Germany and the Czech Republic.

August: AES agreed to pay $376 million to buy out the holdings of its American partner, PSEG Global, in five jointly owned businesses in Argentina: two generation companies and three distribution companies. *Platts Global Power Report* once again named AES the largest equity investor in the global competitive power industry, as it had done every year since 1997. Measured in ownership of hard assets, AES was nearly twice the size of the next largest company.

This, as it turned out, was the high-water mark for AES and the independent power sector.

Under the frenetic activity of deal making all these months had lurked vague worries, which reached the business press, about the financial health of Enron, a major player in the California market and America's largest power trader. Although Enron and AES had been early competitors in the independent electricity sector, Enron had pulled out of the generation business and focused on trading electricity and non-energy commodities, such as digital broadband services, as a broker between suppliers and buyers through forward contracts. The spectacular growth in earnings reported in Enron's financial statements of the late 1990s through the end of 2000 came largely from trading rather than from sales of gas transported in pipelines and electricity generated in its own plants.

Vague worries turned specific soon enough. By the end of the year, the high-flying Enron had fallen into bankruptcy, its finances corrupted with apparent fraud and its senior executives facing criminal indictments. But well before that, the more modest AES had to admit troubles of its own—not in criminal activities but in managerial performance.

On September 25, 2001, AES announced that it would not, after all, achieve the high earnings it had so confidently estimated eight months before. For the first time in a decade of spectacular growth, ever since it had become a public company, AES would fail to meet Wall Street's—and its own—projections. For larger, well-established companies, this would be a disappointing but hardly disastrous development. For a brash young company built on consistent, dramatic growth, it was nearly fatal—and it came in a market

already depressed by the troubles of Enron, just two weeks after the terror-
ist attacks on New York and Washington.

In twenty-four hours, the company's stock price collapsed by nearly 50
percent, on fire-sale volume amounting to about 10 percent of shares outstanding, bringing the AES market valuation down by more than 80 percent since the start of what was supposed to have been another boom year.
Leading investment analysts immediately downgraded their ratings and rec-
ommendations.

In a prepared statement and a conference call with analysts, Bakke
declared the obvious: "This year will be an economic setback for AES." He
blamed the cumulative effect of diverse negative developments: continued
weakening of the Brazilian real; continued decline in electricity prices in
Britain, where AES people in the field had expected them to rise; and the
inability to replace from other new businesses the earnings anticipated from
the aborted Mohave plant. If some of the AES businesses around the world
had performed better than expected, the resulting revenues to the corporation were not enough to offset the negative effects of the others.

Bakke insisted that new projects in development would soon restore his
company's upward trajectory. "We see this essentially as a missed year of earnings growth," he told the analysts. That it certainly was, but many investors
and even directors, officers, and friends of the company wondered if the startling announcement signaled more than a mere speed bump.

The news could hardly have come at a more untimely juncture.
"Confidence in the independent power sector was already eroding that
September," said Sant, looking back,

> from the politically charged issues of power shortages in California and the
> rapid deterioration of Enron and other energy companies engaged in the
> power trading business.
>
> It was only natural for the investing public to ask whether the difficul-
> ties at AES were related to the power trading scandals that had consumed
> Enron. The board was confident from the start that our failures of 2001 were
> not brought about by any attempts to deceive or defraud. This is small con-

solation, however, when your earnings base is deteriorating, and you do not have an immediate response to it.

Trade journals that years before had expressed concern about the possibilities of "nasty surprises" lurking in the independent power sector became almost plaintive in their distress at the Enron-driven rout. An unusual editorial early in 2002 in *Electricity Daily* said that "one of the most troubling aspects of the Enron collapse is the collateral damage"; among the "innocent civilians" listed as injured were Calpine, Dynegy, NRG, Mirant, and "most dramatically, AES." "These companies have little in common with each other or with Enron, other than they swim in the unregulated energy waters." All were hit by plunging stock prices and suspicions of dubious management practices.

"And then there is AES," wrote the editor in a sudden change of mood. "This is the company that basically invented the independent power business and is one of the most upright, innovative, and admirable corporate citizens of America." It would be a tragedy if innovative companies were to expire because of Enron, *Electricity Daily* lamented, "particularly the admirable AES. . . . Let's hope the markets give the company a fair chance."

No such note of sympathy was heard from the tougher Wall Street analysts. "AES's aggressive growth strategy—which hinged on developing new projects around the world—looks like a pipe dream," wrote one *Business Week* commentator. "AES's strategy may still be a good one over the long-term, but in this brutal earnings environment, it may need to spend some time rebuilding confidence among analysts and investors before the stock can rebound."

A few seasoned AES watchers tried to keep the faith. "There are a lot of examples of companies that have got it wrong, that fundamentally haven't done well in the international market," said Hugh Holman of CIBC World Markets to *Business Week*. "AES has done fine. . . . Internationally and domestically, you have to say that AES has the most experience, and probably the best track record in terms of making successes of projects of any of the U.S. companies that have taken on the global market."

But such entrepreneurial confidence faded over the coming weeks. *Energy Daily* reported "substantial skepticism" on Wall Street that AES could maintain "its go-go business model: rapid-fire acquisitions to keep its growth, profits and stock price soaring." A company that had grown accustomed to accessing as much as $6 billion per year in the capital markets found itself with zero access.

Criticism was soon focused on AES' management. For all the specific circumstances bringing about the immediate setback, said Ronald Barone of UBS Warburg, "AES management has lost a significant amount of credibility in the market." Even the supportive Holman wrote bluntly: "This is a top management failure."

The chairman of AES' board of directors, Roger Sant, was reluctantly approaching the same conclusion. The operating values and practices of a small, almost family-like, company simply could not withstand the stresses of such a rapid transformation into a giant multinational.

"We were not going to meet our earnings projections for the first time in nineteen great years," Sant said, looking back on the whole crisis. "From that point on we were engaged in a battle for survival, with the Street, with our investors, our bondholders, our bankers, everyone who had held such faith and confidence in us."

Over months past, independent board members had questioned whether Bakke was in the right role as chief executive officer of a sprawling multinational corporation. He inspired dedication and loyalty among his growing flock of AES people. He was charming, funny, and infectiously committed to the AES management values as he proselytized for them. But from time to time, directors would ask if perhaps something more practical were required of a chief executive officer—headquarters capacities, perhaps, for accountability and financial monitoring of the deals in the field. As they looked back, the directors recalled that Bakke would routinely deflect such discussions.

After the September earnings announcement, the board held a formal meeting to discuss the future executive leadership of the company. Directors asked if Sant would be willing to suspend his philanthropic activities and return to active management as co-CEO alongside Bakke, as it had been in the old days. To the board's dismay, Bakke refused the proposition, and the directors once again settled for a compromise. There would be a division of responsibilities, with Sant returning to full-time status alongside Bakke, joined by four new chief operating officers pulled from the ranks to oversee various parts of the business: Stuart Ryan, Paul Hanrahan, John Ruggirello, and the longtime chief financial officer, Barry Sharp—all of whom had grown up within AES.

At the start of February 2002, AES invited financial analysts to a conference in Florida for two days of management reports on the company's turnaround strategy. Seldom has an analysts' meeting turned into such a rout. Typical of the reactions to the meeting: "We do not believe AES possesses the appropriate commercial skills to manage" the looming risks, from Salomon Smith Barney as it joined other research groups in downgrading AES. Within two weeks, AES stock had dropped to fifty-two-week lows.

Bond-rating agencies downgraded AES paper, already in junk bond territory, which then traded in the dismal range of almost 50 percent below par. The downgrade reflected "concerns about the adequacy of cash flow relative to the large debt load of the company, as well as the stability and predictability of that cash flow," wrote Moody's. UBS Warburg advised clients that the problems at AES "look worse than previously believed."

Sant, Bakke, and top executives held an emotional weekend meeting at the Arlington offices on February 16 and 17, to toughen the turnaround plan. Bakke was quoted in the trade press as acknowledging that people were "a little riled up"—not least of all he himself as he was forced to a forward sale of 7 million shares of his personal AES holdings, margin collateral for a $36 million loan.

Sant and nervous directors determined that outside help was needed and, with Bakke's concurrence, commissioned McKinsey & Company to conduct a strategic diagnosis of AES' position. The board appointed a chief turnaround officer, AES general counsel Bill Luraschi, and called in Lazard Frères & Co. as a financial and restructuring advisor. Seasoned executives know that management consultants can make any situation look bad, but the McKinsey conclusions, when presented on June 5, were far from the reassurance that board members had anticipated.

Even in some of its successful power plants, AES' operating performance lagged behind that of a peer group of the independent power sector—a particularly bitter blow for a company that had prided itself on operational excellence.

AES directors determined that they could no longer delay the appointment of a new chief executive officer. Individually and in ad hoc groups, they prepared diagnostic memos defining specific problems and possible avenues for solutions. Bakke told Sant he was considering resigning. Sant responded that this was the right decision, and proposed that he, too, should resign. "We shared responsibility for destroying so much value in the company," Sant said. "It was time for a new leadership of both CEO and chairman."

The board held an extraordinary Sunday morning meeting on June 16, 2002, at the Pentagon City Ritz-Carlton. Bakke and Sant presented their resignations. Bakke's was accepted; Sant's was not. Instead, directors asked him to delay his retirement for a transitional period of two years, during which he would head AES as a full-time working chairman. The board chose Paul Hanrahan, who had risen through the company ranks to become a chief operating officer, to be president and CEO in Bakke's place. The board also elected a new member, Richard Darman, a friend of the AES founding generation since the era of the energy crisis; Darman quickly fell in line to become the nonexecutive chairman of the company at the conclusion of Sant's two-year transitional leadership.

Bakke was naturally bitter at the loss of support he suffered among company directors, many of whom were longtime friends. He saw them as standing by him in the boom years only to abandon him when the going got rough. In an informal conversation a few weeks later, he loyally avoided singling out individuals for their decisions on that day, but he added, "It will take a long time for some old friendships to be repaired." Indeed, during the tense internal discussions, he threw out the epithet "Brutus!" to one old friend of happier days.

Then, with his associates and staff at AES, some of whom met the news of his departure with tears and themselves talked of resigning, Bakke tried to be upbeat. "AES needs to adjust to a new way of life," he wrote in an e-mailed personal farewell. "While I am proud enough to think I could have adapted, it would not have fit my strengths. . . . [Hanrahan and the new leadership team] can only reach their full potential if I step away. Roger Sant did that for me $8^{1}/_{2}$ years ago, and I am now following in his footsteps."

Sant was also dismayed at the events of June 2002, for some of the same reasons but also for different ones. At the age of seventy-one, he was being asked to turn away from his new career in philanthropy, wherein he supported causes that he and his wife cared deeply about. Instead, he would have to devote himself full-time to business leadership at AES. (The move was no less painful for the fact that the Sants' family foundation, also an AES shareholder, had been decimated by the 2001 debacle, leaving few resources for the ambitious programs they had anticipated.) "I didn't want it anymore," he said in an interview, "but I felt that I couldn't just walk out on the company which we had created and which represented twenty years of my life."

It was not so much the frenetic deals and business strategies of the Bakke era that bothered Sant; those he could have stepped in as board chairman to question, and he had not done so. At the time, he had expressed reluctance to appear to undermine his successor's authority. But later he admitted that he had in fact missed many of the signals of diminishing performance.

Most troubling to him was the subtle shift in AES' culture of values, which Sant and Bakke had evolved from the initial conception of their company long before it became a successful reality. A colleague in the office happened to dig out of a tattered desk file a copy of the memorandum on values that Sant had sent around in the innocent months of 1985 (see chapter 4). Sant remembered writing the memo and knew he must have filed it away somewhere, but he had not the slightest idea where.

Rereading this in the light of all that had followed, Sant could articulate to himself what had worried him, the distortions and exaggerations that the era of dynamic expansion had imposed on the founding values.

"Recontexting" may have seemed a pleasantly appropriate process a decade back, as a little start-up venture made bold to position itself as the Global Power Company. But the dire circumstances of 2002 demanded nothing less than fundamental reconstruction.

Box 10.1

Notes for the Record By Roger Sant (2004)

After Dennis left, we all still felt strongly that our values were the most important part of our company. But I began to see that they had been interpreted in ways contrary to what we had originally intended. To get AES back on the right track, we would have to accomplish a major conversion in our culture: as it had changed in the years of our global expansion, it had become something different from what it was meant to be. Basically, instead of provoking us to guide and measure our actions, the values were becoming rigidly prescriptive of the ways we would do our work.

A few examples: "Integrity" was interpreted to mean that you trust all the people all the time; we never meant to do away with all checks and balances, like a corporate compliance officer or internal audits. "Fairness" didn't mean that everyone was going to keep their jobs, especially with the company in crisis. There were going to be demotions and promotions that some people might not think were fair. Some people were going to lose their jobs; some people would have to change their jobs. "Fairness" did mean that we stood ready with practical support to help them find new jobs and careers.

Then was the matter of "fun." Fun meant the pride we got from our outstanding performance, not just the pushing down of decisions. Giving people the authority to make decisions is neither a substitute for providing leadership and training nor a reason to reduce oversight and accountability. We had seemed to be running with our shared value of "fun" defined as radically decentralized management, the absence of a responsible headquarters staff.

To me, examples like these added up to a misreading and an exaggeration. They marked the difference between a "value" and a "policy." Our CEO had been preaching the gospel that radical decentralization was the backbone of AES. I began to fear that a general cultural value was becoming a prescriptive operating principle.

It came to me gradually: it was like taking a word like "love," and saying, "I now can define what 'love' means and here is how we should do it." We were taking a word like "fun" and defining it: no central staff, no central expertise; the senior leader of the company will only make one decision a year, all decisions will be made by people in the field, the board of directors' major role is to advise, the senior leaders' role is to give up power. Declarations of purpose (serving the world) and fun (here is the money; use it as you think best) superseded the clear holding of people accountable for their actions, and clear audits necessary to make something like this work.

If we brought in that accountability and oversight, would the human characteristics of our culture, the humanity in the organization which many people felt was unique, be lost? I believe that this is not necessarily the way it has to come out. Focusing on performance, focusing on excellence can increase the humanity of the company. Performance doesn't have to be achieved in a dog-eat-dog or confrontational environment, though in too many other companies that is what happens.

In the turnaround of our company, we would have to ensure that the people of AES understood that specific, operational interpretation of our values had to be dropped. We would continue to invoke our values, in their broadest, most provocative forms, not in their narrowest, most prescriptive form. Being compassionate, caring and respectful of the situations and people around us would not conflict with expectations of performance.

ELEVEN

Turnaround

In the enthusiasm of growing ever bigger, of serving the visionary cause of bringing a better life to people the world over, the AES leadership had grown lax, careless in management and undisciplined in disbursing the funds that the financial markets were only too willing to lend. None of the executive venality that undermined Enron was ever a factor, but managerial misjudgments were almost as costly to the company's shareholders.

Common stock that had traded above $70.00 in mid-2000 hit a low in October 2002 at the dangerous and humiliating price of $0.92 per share. (A good moment, for those of iron stomach, to buy: seven months later, the share price had soared to $8.00.) Bondholders were ready to accept as little as $0.30 on the dollar to get whatever money they could out of their holdings. AES lost all access to world capital markets, which had so eagerly fueled its dramatic growth during the 1990s.

Wall Street analysts and the company's own consultants and directors combed through the financial statements in detail, noticing at long last that the revenues from more than half of the ambitious electricity projects around the world were coming in at less than the cost of the capital borrowed to develop them. The aggressive buildup of generation capacity from 1997 to 2001 had left AES with a huge burden of debt, and the cash flow to cover the payments was highly suspect.

There was no way around it: in mid-2002 AES was a textbook candidate for bankruptcy.

All the old complaints, muffled during the boom years, came out again, at high volume. Hardened brokers, never having overcome their irritation at Dennis Bakke's preaching of values and virtues during financial discussions, complained. A competitor in the industry scoffed at AES: "This company is just a religious cult!" Loyal AES people recognized their vulnerability. One candid executive told the consultants who were assessing the company that negotiating strategies at all levels were often casual, sometimes almost careless, even in complex financing matters. "AES is pretty much viewed as sheep ripe for the fleecing," he concluded. The enthusiasm of the people in the field too often carried the day and the deal; specialized review of performance from headquarters came too late, if at all.

But, beneath the carping and crowd psychology, it took little scrutiny to discover that AES had solid book value. Its assets were hard assets, power plants and distribution companies actually in business—not the illusory trading profits on paper of the sort that brought down the likes of Enron. To be sure, some of the hard assets in the AES portfolio had been overvalued in the enthusiasm of the boom years, and some were indeed underperforming. These faltering projects included many of the huge ventures of 1996 to 2000, into which AES had sunk more than $10 billion of its own accumulated capital instead of adhering to the original financing methods that required each business to stand on its own. Overall, too many long-term assets had been financed on short-term credit; revenues intended to service hard-currency borrowings were denominated in soft currency, subject to inevitable fluctuations in exchange rates.

In short, ever dedicated to providing electricity to needy populations, the company inspired by Roger Sant and Dennis Bakke seemed to neglect such mundane business considerations as cash flow and return on invested capital, in favor of abstract cultural values.

All of this was apparent in the summer of 2002, when Paul Hanrahan, a sixteen-year AES veteran, took over operations from the founders (though the board prevailed on Sant to remain as full-time but unpaid executive chairman).

Hanrahan would tackle the task that he knew best: develop a turnaround strategy for a vulnerable and underperforming business. There was no talk of mere "recontexting." In sadness and apprehension, Sant muttered at one point, "It's going to turn out to be a totally different company, no doubt about it."

Bakke, the more injured of the cofounders, did not fight this judgment. "AES needs a different kind of leadership than it did in the past," he said as he announced his resignation. "What will be needed for the foreseeable future will be leaders who are inclined toward efficiency, discipline, accountability and control"—qualities that he admitted he had "gagged on" during the buoyant years of his leadership. "By retiring from the CEO role at this time I want to model the kind of accountability to which leaders should be held. The economic performance of AES during the past year has been dreadful. As its leader, I take full responsibility."

In fact and fairness—and the clear vision of hindsight—AES' real economic performance had been dreadful for longer than just one bad year. And Bakke did not need to assume full responsibility; there was plenty to be spread around.

The obvious first step toward turnaround would have to be success in cleaning up the parent company's balance sheet, reducing the dangerous leverage of a huge debt overhang and presenting enough liquidity that investors would be willing to rejoin the company.

Back in the glory years of unfettered growth, when debt capital flowed in merrily, the AES management showed few qualms about accepting early maturity dates for repayment. No matter, went the reasoning; there would be plenty of cash flow and revenues from continued growth to repay the loans. Under the changed circumstances of 2002, Sant and Hanrahan were sobered by the realization that during 2003 no less than $1.3 billion would have to be either repaid in cash or refinanced to stretch out the maturity dates.

Cost cutting in operations and postponement of capital expenditures for future development could help, but only so far. At least six plants and businesses could be identified right away as underperforming, including enterprises of high visibility but dubious prospects, such as the Bujagali

Falls dam development project in Uganda, the fabled distribution company in the Republic of Georgia, and the huge Drax Power Station in northern England.

Drax, a showpiece business, had fallen on hard times when its major customer, the European subsidiary of the former Texas Utilities, the TXU Corporation, went out of business. Critics of AES often cited Drax as a prime example of the company "ripe for the fleecing." AES had paid much too much for it, they said, in 1999, about $3 billion. By 2005, when the struggling plant was finally put out for auction, the winning bid came in at more than $3.5 billion, going far to justify AES' original purchase price. Unfortunately, of course, the precarious AES balance sheet had long since forced the company to walk away from Drax and turn it over to the creditors. Any satisfaction at the ultimate sale could be only psychological, not financial.

Selling of assets for current needs is always a messy process, in a company as in a household. But skillfully managed, it need not degenerate into a fire sale. In the course of 2002, AES realized some $800 million in asset sales and could identify another $1 billion in properties that could command respectable prices.

AES was hardly the only company in the unregulated power sector struggling to escape from the leverage remaining after rapid growth, but it was a prominent case study. Outside financial analysts, such as the Fitch Global Power Group, noted that AES was the first of these endangered independent power producers to successfully refinance and reenter the private equity markets. Christopher Ellinghaus of the Williams Capital Group told the *Washington Post* in mid-2003 that AES might still have to sell more assets, "but I really didn't expect them to make this much progress so quickly."

The parent company reduced its debt by $1.2 billion in 2002. In all, fourteen facilities were sold, in Africa, the Middle East, Asia, Europe, and the United States, bringing in proceeds of $1.1 million. Richard Darman, who would succeed Sant as chairman in mid-2003, explained that the key "was not just selling businesses that could realize good value in a difficult market. It was also avoiding the sale of businesses that are essential to our business strategy."

Skeptics questioned, for example, how AES could expect to profit in underdeveloped markets such as in Pakistan, Kazakhstan, and Georgia. The Sant-Hanrahan management agreed about dim prospects in the former Soviet Georgia but fought doggedly to sustain the businesses in Pakistan and Kazakhstan. Facilities in both countries scored marked improvement, even profitability, in the first years of turnaround.

The power plant Ekibastuz in Kazakhstan is one of the largest coal-fired plants in the world. Under AES management, its operational capacity has increased fourfold. The communist-era management never succeeded in collecting more than 30 percent of its billings, in a culture in which not paying electricity bills was a routine practice. Under AES, with prodding and persuasion, the collection rates have reached almost 100 percent. AES generates heat and electricity for half a million people in Kazakhstan and almost as many in central Russia.

Brazil presented an interesting situation. Political and economic conditions alike thwarted the early promise of the huge AES commitment, and even in Dennis Bakke's time there was talk that AES might decide to pull up stakes and move somewhere more welcoming.

The AES Brazilian subsidiaries had an outstanding loan of $1.2 billion from the Brazilian development bank, BNDES, a major line in the company's heavy debt obligations. Early in 2003, the AES companies defaulted on their scheduled payments; no cash flow was coming in from the Brazilian operations. AES was deep in negotiations to refinance the loan, to stretch out the maturity dates so that the Brazilian power plants and distribution companies could continue in operation under AES management and return to profitability. Given the defaults, however, populist pressures mounted in Brazil, culminating in the demand that the state bank take over ownership of the AES holdings.

Wall Street analysts familiar with the AES balance sheet did not hesitate to go public with the discovery of a remarkable anomaly. As an analyst from Blaylock & Partners told the *Washington Post* (which was closely watching the fate of its hometown company across the river in Arlington), the Brazilian subsidiaries were carried as $5 billion in assets, against liabilities of $6 billion. If AES were to abandon its Brazilian businesses, both sides of the ledger would be damaged, but the company's balance sheet would actually be strengthened. As for the AES income statement, for the moment there was no income coming in anyway—just losses.

"This put us in a rather strong negotiating position," Sant said wryly. Eventually a successful restructuring was hammered out, led by a newcomer to the AES executive corps, Joe Brandt. The AES Brazilian enterprise gradually gained in strength, moving toward becoming the broadly successful electricity business that had been anticipated from the start.

For all the headquarters' focus on restoring liquidity to the balance sheet, Hanrahan, the new chief executive officer, forty-six years old, still had a global power business to run, with the normal problems that arise in a large multinational corporation engaged in a dynamic and rapidly developing heavy industry.

AES operated three aging power plants in Hungary, for example, relics of Soviet economic development. In 2002, postcommunist Hungary was preparing to join the European Union (EU). Among other entry requirements were environmental standards far higher than the country had known under communism. As they stood, the three plants would have to be shut down by 2004.

AES engineers determined that one of the plants could be retrofitted and operated in compliance with the new regulations, but the other two, burning low-quality brown coal to produce electricity, seemed hopeless. Learning from the company's experience in California and elsewhere, the Hungarian managers jumped at a proposal to convert the two old plants from burning coal exclusively to burning biomass, wood, and a combination of wood and coal. This held the promise of markedly curtailing noxious emissions, bringing the AES businesses close to EU compliance and earning a reduction, going forward, in the country's environmental tax.

The savings from this tax reduction made an investment in environmental responsibility feasible. Just these two AES biomass plants now provide one-third of Hungary's total renewable energy. Sulfur dioxide and dust emissions have decreased by 90 percent, carbon dioxide emissions by more than 80 percent.

The company's management style and its culture remained at the heart of Sant's concerns. There came to be less talk of values, a conscious decision of the new leadership. If, they insisted, none of the deep-seated values need be relinquished, AES people chose not to talk about them as much. Even Sant conceded in an interview, "Maybe we were too 'in-your-face' about all that."

But could the culture and style of a family business be maintained? If the values were not to be talked about as much, would they also not be thought about as much?

Toward the end of 2005, the investment community of Wall Street became more positive about AES than at any time since the bubble's burst. Citing the potential for above-average earnings growth and an improved balance sheet, Standard & Poor's analysts rated AES stock a "strong buy." Others may not have been quite that certain, but "buy" was clearly the prevailing word.

Industry analyst Gary F. Hovis wrote a comprehensive assessment for the Argus Research Company:

> AES is finally back on track. . . . After a length of time in which the company was brought to the edge of a Chapter 11 bankruptcy filing, our analysis shows that AES is now starting to move ahead and leave behind its myriad of problems. . . . We think AES has thus far been quite successful in moving forward with its short-term bank loan refinancing program and, most important of all, shows a much improved liquidity position.
>
> The company is now making strong progress toward optimizing the value of its generating portfolio to produce above-average returns over the long term. . . . We think the company's platform for a return to strong growth is solid, and are confident in management's ability to provide shareholders with the increased value.

Not for quite a few years had AES people been able to read such comments about their work. Insiders and outsiders alike well knew that the competitive generation and distribution of electricity had been and always would be a risky business; a number of competitors from the early boom years had fallen by the wayside.

Shortly after Roger Sant retired, for the second time, in 2003, he allowed himself the luxury of reflecting on the lessons of the AES experience. He was confident that Hanrahan and the second generation of leaders were taking hold effectively. The balance sheet was being repaired; faltering projects were being shed, written off, or turned around; and operating performance was being improved. Indeed, evidence was growing that the financial community recognized this reality—that AES was no Enron, that it remained a viable multinational business, if still well short of the inflated expectations of a few years before.

AES became the largest international power company in the world on the basis of megawatts owned and controlled, number of countries served, and percentage of capacity beyond its home country; 90 percent of the company's people live and work outside the United States. AES operates in twenty-seven countries on five continents, with the capacity to serve the electricity needs of 100 million of the world's people.

In the glory years of growth and enthusiasm, Sant often brushed aside calls for caution, arguing, "If we're in the electricity business, we have to go where the demand is." Confronting the stresses of rapid growth and financial implosion, he feared that AES might have to become a totally different company. As it played out, one of the fundamental decisions of the new management during the turnaround period was that AES would remain a global power company—it would not settle in, as many of its competitors had done, to a comfortable market close to home.

As this book goes to press, in early 2007, numerous studies project a sharply growing demand for electricity worldwide, certainly over the coming generation but also in the next five years. AES is already operating and marketing where 60 percent of this energy growth is expected to occur.

Still going where the demand is, maybe the AES "reenergized" after the crisis of 2001 will not be such a different company after all. It may simply be rediscovering its roots, and cultivating them with the nourishment of experience.

EPILOGUE

By Roger Sant

"The AES system is designed to make sure power is distributed throughout the organization." That is what we said to the *Harvard Business Review* back in 1999, and I still think the model served us well, with many positive outcomes.

In hindsight, however, I can only admit the obvious, that our business model didn't work as well as we hoped it would, especially when it was stressed by our rapid growth. Essentially, what we did was take a plausible and workable model and then exaggerate it, take it to extremes–breaking the back, finally, of the ideas that underlay the model in the first place.

So what did we learn, and how and when did we learn it?

The mid-1990s was the beginning of an extraordinary growth period for AES. It was then that we departed from the traditions of our first fifteen years, when there had been a good deal of discipline regarding empowerment within the company.

As our growth increased, we began to work in a less disciplined atmosphere to keep it going. Things began to happen too fast. Partly as a result of the business climate, almost any viable company–particularly one that, like ours, was flying high–had access to capital. It was increasingly hard for any of us to say, "Let's pass up some of these opportunities; let's ration ourselves, let's control ourselves, let's discipline ourselves."

We stuck to the notion that if there was a good project, we could find the money. In hindsight, I am convinced that our fault was not so much in taking advantage of the robust capital markets—the ready access to equity and debt capital in those years. What was missing was our earlier discipline in defining good projects.

So the first lesson of our hindsight is that we didn't have enough accountability for ourselves. There was little tracking of performance after decisions were made. Giving a person the responsibility to make decisions is a good thing. But our not following up to see how those decisions played out in actual performance left people unconcerned about the consequences of poor analysis. Almost no one lost a job; almost no one was demoted; almost no one was docked in pay. Too often, decisions were made at a level well below the competence necessary to make those decisions.

A second lesson was in our compensation practice, principally in giving bonuses for closing deals. The entire reward system was based on closing the deal, not on the performance of the deal once it had been closed. This motivated a few irresponsible actions. It was argued over and over that the reason we were growing so fast was that we were closing a lot of deals. Clearly, the closing of a deal was the rewarded behavior. In our culture, the people who were closing deals were the people of high visibility.

Third, instead of any kind of corporate-level approval for a new business, we had what we called an "advice" process. A team would develop a project and put the arguments together in an "advice paper" (these varied radically in quality and insight), and then others in the company, peers as well as superiors, would offer comments from their own experience. Even the board was eventually persuaded that it was there just to give advice, not to approve or disapprove projects—though the board could always register its degree of confidence in each project team.

For a time this worked. The breakdown came, we can now see, as people began to take the advice requests less than seriously; there grew a lack of honesty, an unwillingness to discourage peer developers or peer executives. And there just was not enough time to do an adequate job of review.

For one thing, we had no functional specialists–experts, say, in risk management or financial modeling. I know, I glibly told the *Harvard Business Review* that we liked to "reinvent the wheel" whenever we had the chance–such was our bias against experts in one thing or another.

But as our notion played out, it meant that people submitting proposals were not getting the benefit of responses like "I think you can do this better" and "Have you looked into this?" Instead came back anecdotal or perhaps irrelevant experiences, of dubious help to the people promoting the new projects. Often these were enthusiastic and "empowered" people who had very little apprenticeship or training, so they were forging ahead with their own blinders in place. And I have to say that because aspects of the model were pushed too far, a small minority of people created some huge problems by taking personal advantage of our trust.

Because we were growing so rapidly, all of our new people were coming in from acquisitions. We no longer recruited people from colleges and business schools, because the new businesses we acquired each year had people who we thought we should use in the company–many of whom didn't have any of the background for business development that we assumed.

In a decentralized or "empowered" organization, the most important component is mutual trust. Trust has to be developed; it does not come overnight. A lot of the people new to AES came from environments where trust was not as important as it was to us. Yet we threw them into a culture where trust was the principal component for success. This is just an example of what I mean by saying that we "exaggerated" our culture.

In our years of phenomenal growth, the responsible corporate center got relatively smaller and smaller. The revenues of AES, the market capitalization, the balance sheet, grew in the 1990s by factors of 10 or 100; the corporate staff didn't grow at all. Dennis Bakke, as chief executive officer, made a point of declaring that he made only one decision per year. I understood the point he was making, and his rhetorical style, but I am still embarrassed to think that a statement like that would be a source of pride.

We were always proud of the full and frequent flow of detailed company information that we passed on to our people, wherever they were. It got to the point that securities lawyers declared each and every AES person to be an "insider" when it came to purchases and sales of company stock. That's all true; we really did try to do everything we could to make information available to everyone and thus encourage them to be knowledgeable about the company, to be insiders.

The bad part was not that we were sharing information but that the shared information lacked some fairly crucial fundamental metrics: return on invested capital, benchmark comparisons with other companies in our sector, calculation of weighted average cost of capital. We used the same weighted cost of capital–or discount rate–for a project in the Republic of Georgia as we did for a project in the state of Georgia. We didn't provide the information that would give people appropriate insights. If we had conveyed more of a sense of how we were creating value during those years, we would have been much better served than by merely recording completion of deals.

We were missing a capital allocation process at the center, a means of comparing project against project. Without a formal approval process, there wasn't enough formality in the system to make it serious. We were lacking a risk management function to help evaluate commodity risk, interest rate risk, country risk, and political risk–a function that was added, to our benefit, during our later turnaround. Such risks can never be precisely determined, but there are ways of quantifying them; more rigorous risk analysis would have helped in building hedges.

All of these things were normal procedure in the early days when we had no capital. Before we could get lenders to finance a project, we had to go through every risk they could bring up, and have an answer for it. The more risks we were able to handle, the higher the financing percentage would be. As time went on, we didn't bother with that as much because we could use corporate capital in larger percentages of each project.

Over time, we let our corporate balance sheet grow without any strong sense of financial strategy. Back when I taught my students at the Stanford Graduate School of Business about corporate finance, we had a lot of fun trying to figure out the optimal financial strategy, the optimal balance sheet, the optimal relationship between debt and equity.

At AES, we eventually just ignored this discussion and convinced ourselves to "let it be what it's going to be." We let facile sayings creep in, like "Debt is always cheaper than equity." We probably all knew better, and yet we let it continue. We knew there comes a point at which that premise is exactly wrong–where the risk of more debt is more costly than adding equity. If we had emphasized analysis and provided rigorous training, or even mentoring, at the corporate level, we would have done much better work.

I've wondered, what if we had just stuck with our original financial model, the nonrecourse-debt model that we used for the first fifteen years? Bakke used to say, "Every tub on its own bottom." That meant that the only debt AES would incur would be linked to a specific project, to its revenues and cash flow. Each business would be financed on its own creditworthiness so that the only corporate capital at risk was the very modest equity investment.

If, in 1996, we had stuck to the rule that each project must be financed on its own, we might have been able to keep the decentralized structure of our culture. The need to create a corporate center was a direct result of our incurring corporate debt to contribute the equity investment required in risky projects. We should have debated this turn more vigorously.

If all these reflections are right, then it finally comes back to the roles of the senior leaders, the group managers and the other senior people in the company who saw their principal roles as (1) encouraging people to find new projects and (2) inculcating the AES culture, the values.

Those two roles are essential, but they alone are insufficient. Training and development, data and controls on cash flows, expectations of greater accountability, excellent recruiting–these are examples of other responsibilities of leadership. Visits by company leaders to AES plants and businesses became discussions of values; fundamental performance metrics were ignored. Even safety and environmental performance were given little attention in favor of broader discussions of social responsibility. Things we all believed in were being exaggerated at the expense of sensible management controls.

In an empowered organization, the essence of leadership is not abdication of responsibility. It's actually the assumption of a greater burden of responsibility. The responsibility shifts from making and/or reviewing decisions to the critical task of developing, training, and mentoring the decision makers; selecting the right leaders for the right decisions and allocating the decision rights very carefully; and monitoring performance and responding appropriately. This amounts to a much more nuanced leadership responsibility.

By the beginning of 2006, AES' market capitalization had climbed back up to $11.5 billion and shares were trading close to $20.00. The company's bonds, which had once traded as low as $0.30 on the dollar, were back up to par and selling even at a premium above the par value—this was one of my main financial goals, as a solid measure of turnaround. We had solid projections for double-digit revenue growth in the years to come.

After our retrenchments and refinancings, we were again able to commit to new businesses—power plants in Spain, Bulgaria, and elsewhere. And we were able to enter the business of renewable sources of energy, so long desired but so long elusive in economic viability. Global demand for wind power is expected to grow by more than 15 percent annually. AES acquired a small developer and operator of wind farms, SeaWest, operating in California, Wyoming, and Oregon, with further development sites in other western states. We also bought an equity interest in US Wind Force, a private company in the eastern United States with development sites for wind farms in various stages of progress.

With financial turnaround accomplished under CEO Paul Hanrahan came an obvious season for generational turnaround of key personnel, many of whom had been with the company for two decades. Barry Sharp, for twenty years chief financial officer, and author of so many of the "fixes" that saved the company, decided that he had done his part, as did John Ruggirello, mainstay of generation operations since the olden days at Beaver Valley, and Shahzad Qasim, the AES veteran leading Europe and the Middle East.

From inside and outside the company came new people to fill their places. Andres Gluski, former head of the Venezuelan businesses, now heads all operations in Latin America. From his base in our China operations, Haresh Jaisinghani now heads all the Asian businesses. New to AES are David Gee, a former McKinsey & Company consultant, heading the North American operation; the new chief financial officer is Victoria Harker, previously CFO at MCI.

Similarly, the board of directors has undergone a transition. Serving with the new chairman, Dick Darman, are holdover directors John McArthur, Philip Lader, and until May of 2006, me. We have recruited an impressive slate of six new independent directors: Sven Sandstrom, former deputy director of the World Bank; Charles Rossotti, former head of the Internal Revenue Service; Kristina Johnson, dean of Duke University's Pratt School of Engineering; Philip Odeen, former CEO of TRW; John Koskinen, former deputy mayor of Washington, DC; and Sandra Moose, a former partner at the Boston Consulting Group.

In sum, many of the AES officers and directors who experienced the fall of company stock from $70.00 to $1.00 are gone. Into their places have come promising new leaders whose experience with the company is the growth of the stock price from $1.00 to $20.00, with it poised for still more. In this, as in so many other factors, AES is finding a new context.

A final perspective at the end of 2006: In the fifteen and a half years since AES had its 1991 public offering, the total return of the S&P index is up 420 percent. Over the same period, AES shares are up 612 percent.

INDEX

Note: *plates* refer to photographs in the color insert

AES Board of Directors, Past and Present

Roger W. Sant (1981–2006): Cofounder and Chairman Emeritus of AES Corporation.

Thomas I. Unterberg (1981–2002): Founder, Chairman and Senior Advisor, C.E. Unterberg, Towbin Holdings, Inc.

John E. Bryson (1982–1985): Chairman, President and Chief Executive Officer, Edison International

C. Arthur Rolander (1982–1993): Former Senior Vice President of Gulf Oil Corporation; Former President of General Atomic Company and General Atomic International.

Russell E. Train (1982–1997): Founder Chairman Emeritus, World Wildlife Fund U.S.; former Administrator, U.S. Environmental Protection Agency.

Frank Jungers (1983–2002): Retired Chairman of the Board and Chief Executive Officer of the Arabian American Oil Company.

Robert H. Waterman Jr. (1985–2002): Co-author of *In Search of Excellence,* and the author of several other best-selling books on management including: *The Renewal Factor, Adhocracy–The Power to Change, and What America Does Right;* former Partner, McKinsey & Company.

Dennis W. Bakke (1986–2002): Cofounder and President Emeritus of AES Corporation.

Henry R. Linden (1987–1997): Max McGraw Professor of Energy and Power Engineering and Management and Director, IIT Energy + Power Center; former President, Gas Research Institute.

Hazel O'Leary (1988–1989, 1997–2002): President, Fisk University; Secretary of the U.S. Department of Energy from 1993 to 1997.

Alice F. Emerson (1993–2004): Former Senior Advisor at the Andrew W. Mellon Foundation; former President of Wheaton College.

Vicki-Ann Assevero (1994–1997): Former Partner with the law firm Holland & Knight.

Robert F. Hemphill Jr. (1996–2003): Executive Vice President of AES Corporation; Former Deputy Manager of Power of the Tennessee Valley Authority.

John H. McArthur (1997–Present): Dean Emeritus, Harvard University Graduate School of Business.

Philip Lader (2001–Present): Chairman, WPP Group plc; Senior Advisor, Morgan Stanley; former US Ambassador to the Court of St. James's.

Richard Darman (2002–Present): Partner and Managing Director, The Carlyle Group; former Director, U.S. Office of Management and Budget.

Paul T. Hanrahan (2002–Present): President and Chief Executive Officer, AES Corporation.

Sven Sandstrom (2002–Present): Director and Treasurer, the International Union for the Conservation of Nature; former Managing Director, The World Bank.

Philip A. Odeen (2003–Present): Non-executive Chairman, Reynolds and Reynolds Company; former Chairman of TRW Inc.; former President and Chief Executive Officer of BDM.

Charles O. Rossotti (2003–Present): Senior Advisor, The Carlyle Group; former Commissioner of the U.S. Internal Revenue Service; former Founder and Chairman, American Management Systems, Inc.

Kristina M. Johnson (2004–Present): Dean, the Edmund T. Pratt Jr. School of Engineering, Duke University.

John A .Koskinen (2004–Present): President, The U.S. Soccer Foundation; former Deputy Mayor and City Administrator, the District of Columbia; former President and CEO, the Palmieri Company.

Sandra O. Moose (2004–Present): President, Strategic Advisory Services LLC; former Senior Vice President and Director, The Boston Consulting Group.